For Better or For Worse

For Better or For Worse

Vietnamese International Marriages in the New Global Economy

Hung Cam Thai

Rutgers University Press
New Brunswick, New Jersey, and London

LIBRARY OF CONGRESS CATALOGING-IN-PUBLICATION DATA

Thai, Hung Cam, 1976–
    For better or for worse: Vietnamese international marriages in the
new global economy / Hung Cam Thai.
        p.   cm.
    Includes bibliographical references and index.
    ISBN 978–0-8135–4288–1 (hardcover : alk. paper)—ISBN 978–0-
8135–4289–8 (pbk. : alk. paper)
    1. Marriage.   2. Vietnamese diaspora [proposed]   3. United
States—Emigration and immigration.   4. Globalization—Social
aspects.   I. Title.
    HQ525.V54T53 2008
    306.84′508995922073—dc22   2007024987

A British Cataloging-in-Publication record for this book is available
from the British Library.

Visit our Web site: http://rutgerspress.rutgers.edu

Manufactured in the United States of America

For my parents,
Pham Thi Lien and Thai Van Hoang

Contents

Preface
The intimate details of globalization

Fifteen years after my family and I left Vietnam as boat refugees, I returned to the country as a young adult on a personal and an intellectual journey to understand transnational lives—personal because in my adulthood I discovered my own transnational connections there, and intellectual because of my childhood in rural America. My family had lived in refugee camps for three years in Thailand and the Phillipines prior to arriving in the United States in early 1982, when I was six years old. I grew up in the housing projects of Pass Christian, a small town on the gulf coast of Mississippi, where I was deeply intrigued early on by the intimate constraints among two groups of people in my environment: the few Asian people I knew and the black female friends I had. As a college student of sociology and gender studies, I took every course that was offered on family and marriage; and in every paper I wrote, I would write about black single motherhood. I was interested in studying the contexts of marriageability, or lack thereof, among black single mothers, because a very close friend in high school became a teenage mother on her own, remaining single and later becoming a pharmacist—a life path that, according to her, made it difficult to find a partner. I aspired to write a book about marriage that would focus on individuals like my close friend—highly educated black women who had relatively few highly educated black men in their marriage markets.

My intention to study black single motherhood changed when, in the winter of 1996, I received a call from someone in Vietnam who claimed to be my mother, from whom I had been separated since the age of three. My parents divorced in postwar Vietnam, and my father subsequently took custody of his children, remaining in his village in the Mekong Delta, while my mother returned to her natal family in a village six hours away. My mother regularly returned to visit my siblings and me in our village. But we lost touch with my mother when my father took us with him, unbeknownst to my mother, as boat refugees in late 1979. Once we arrived in the United States, after spending three years in refugee camps, we did not have any communications with her; Vietnam was closed to most of the world until the early 1990s, making it virtually impossible for Vietnamese in exile to communicate with their families from the late 1970s until the early 1990s. I grew up with a very clear understanding that there was no hope of reuniting with my mother, and early on in my life, my siblings and I were told that my mother had died while trying to flee the country on her own.

I later learned that my mother, in fact, had not passed away and that she managed, after many years of investigative work, to get hold of our contact information through her former social networks from my father's village. After I received a phone call from her in the winter of 1996, I returned to Vietnam to visit for the first time in the summer of 1997, eighteen years after separating from her. I arrived during a time when overseas Vietnamese people, or Viet Kieu, as they are known in Vietnam (Long 2004), had just begun to return in large numbers since the mass exodus of Vietnamese people during the postwar years. At this time, I remained interested in issues of marriageability, but I changed my focus because I wanted to spend more time living in Vietnam, to be with my mother. During my first visit to Vietnam since I had left the country as a child, the moment when my interest in writing this book was crystallized occurred one afternoon in late June 1997, when I met a local group of four wealthy Vietnamese men in Saigon; in their early and mid-twenties themselves, they thought I had returned to Vietnam for a wife.[1]

I was reading at a small upscale café near the central business district when the group of men approached me and asked where I came from, a question I frequently receive when I go to Vietnam, and which implies that I could be from one of many countries that make up the aging Vietnamese diaspora. In Saigon, it is unusual for people to go alone to public venues like cafés and restaurants, and so I stood out because I was by myself. The four men sat across from my table and after exchanging some unfriendly looks, one of them came to my table and started a conversation, followed by the other three. One of the men asked me where I came from, what I did for a living, and how long I had been in Vietnam. I told them that I had returned to meet my mother, and that I wanted to learn more about Vietnamese culture. One of them immediately commented that all I wanted to do was to meet young, beautiful local women in Saigon, and to "take all the good girls to the United States." Taken by surprise because I do not embody any notion of a hegemonic man (Connell 1995) and, at least in the United States and up to this point in my life, had never been viewed as a womanizer. I asked why they thought all I wanted to do was meet beautiful young women. One of them began to explain that all the beautiful local women, who they assumed were all poor, were "selling" themselves to Viet Kieu men, who they assumed were all rich. I then told them that I was dating a woman in the United States, to which they said it did not matter. One man said, "All of you come to Vietnam leaving your wives and girlfriends overseas and just 'play around.'" I asked these men if they could give me examples of people they knew who specifically fit into their descriptions, and if they could introduce me to some of those men; I was attempting to get at specific names of people because I wanted to know how true the stereotype of overseas Vietnamese men was, and if, in fact, these men had kept track of people they knew personally who were in the social situations they thought I was seeking. When I asked this, they were unable to name one specific man they knew who was in Vietnam to "play around" with beautiful local women, women who they claimed were "selling" themselves to such men.

One of the men began to use profanity, ranting about how I made up the excuse of visiting my mother, and that I was just like all the other overseas Vietnamese men who returned to use their status as a Viet Kieu for short-term (sexual) affairs with local women, or that I was there to "buy" a beautiful wife. The conversation got intense, and while his reactions helped me understand the discourse around international intimacy and economic exchanges, I became offended at his intolerable vulgarity, and had to decide whether or not to stay and learn more about his reactions. In fieldwork, as I quickly learned, the researcher has to decide how much to tolerate from potential informants for the sake of data. When I felt too uncomfortable with the conversation, I decided to leave the café, but I left frustrated, and with several immediate questions. How true was the stereotype about overseas Vietnamese men who returned for short-term sexual affairs with women in Vietnam or to "buy" beautiful wives? How true was the implication that women in Vietnam were "selling" themselves, engaging in sex work, or generally taking part in international intimacy for the simple exchange of money, whether or not sex was involved?

What I learned through the exchange with the four men at the café, then, was that there were strong beliefs among some locals in Vietnam about the sexual and economic exchanges between local women and overseas men, including Viet Kieu and other foreigners. But their belief was that overseas men were just there, at best, to meet beautiful young women to have short-term affairs for the exchange of money, and at worst, were using their first-world status and image to dupe local women for free sex. I wanted to see if this was true, and if it was, there was an important sociological story to tell about this corner of the global intimate economy.[2] In using the term *intimate* economy, I share Ara Wilson's notion that it comprises the "feature of people's lives that have come to seem noneconomic, particularly social identities (e.g. woman) and relationships (e.g. kinship)" (2004, 11). I wanted to understand how men and women in this cultural corner experience the double meaning of what Sherry Ortner calls "making gender," that is how they are "constructed by, and subjected to, the cultural and historical discourses within which they must operate," as well as how they "enact, resist, or negotiate the world as given, and in so doing 'make' the world" (1996, 1).

In the end, after spending fourteen (discontinuous) months of fieldwork in Vietnam and in the United States between June 1997 and March 2001 to collect evidence for this book, I did encounter overseas men who visited Saigon for short-term emotionless sexual liaisons, and I also met plenty of women there who were engaged in sex work with clients from overseas for the simple exchange of money, as well as other women who found ways to meet foreigners, including Viet Kieu men, for marriage as a strategy for migration. But this dichotomous finding constituted only a small portion of what I saw in the social spaces where Viet Kieu men and local women converged, and to claim that it was the only, or even the dominant pattern, of this intimate economy would be inaccurate. I quickly found out that there were different markets of intimacy, depending on people's migration histories, transnational networks, and contexts of return from the diaspora.

This book, therefore, is about one facet of these complicated intimate details of globalization. I do not aspire to document and, in fact, refrain from documenting all the possibilities of a global intimate economy in Vietnam and in the Vietnamese diaspora. Instead, in the chapters that follow, I document key processes embedded in the recent formation of an international marriage market linking women in Vietnam and overseas Vietnamese men living in Western countries. This task is particularly important because these international marriages follow a global trend that has been gathering momentum over the past forty years: immigrant and immigrant-origin people, especially men, are more and more frequently seeking spouses in their countries of origin. Why, I am asking, do men and women in different corners of the Vietnamese diaspora globally expand their marriage options? In presenting case studies of particular marriages, I offer an exploratory look at the connections between personal, material, and social factors that explain why immigrants return to their home countries for marriage as well as the reasons that motivate those from the homeland to seek international migration for marriage or international marriage for migration. My approach is to provide an analysis that is suffused with personal subjectivities in underscoring processes of transnationalism, conceptualized as the process by which immigrants build and maintain social and economic ties with their home countries after they migrate overseas (Basch, Glick Schiller, and Szanton Blanc 1994; Glick Schiller, Basch, and Blanc Szanton 1992).

I tell the story of uniting with my mother and the moment that crystallized my interest in writing this book in order to provide the background and context for understanding my role in this transnational project. Because I had never returned to Vietnam for a spouse, and no one in my network of kin was involved in an international marriage at the time I did the research, it was not an issue that directly affected my life at that time. I was relatively unfamiliar with key processes of international marriage migration in the Vietnamese diaspora except for the gossip, rumors, speculations—and mostly myths—that I had heard from family, friends, and strangers who knew people on the international marriage market. Indeed, reflecting viewpoints like those behind the altercation I had with the young men at the café in Saigon, the limited literature on international marriage migration is often carelessly reduced to stories about economic exploitation and construed in larger discussions on the global trafficking of women (Enloe 2000; Glodava and Onizuka 1994; Tolentino 1996).

I have found that Nicole Constable has offered one of the most important insights on international marriages in her study of mail-order brides from China and the Philippines. She cautions that international marriages in the new global economy should not be understood as a "simple unilinear movement from East to West, from underdeveloped 'South' to developed 'North,' from so-called traditional societies to so-called modern ones, or from oppression to liberation" (2003, 165). As a matter of fact, I agree with Denise Brennan's assertion that in studying transnational networks, "we must address the issue of differential power held by various actors within the transnational social field, a power delimited not just by differences in class, gender, and race but also by the relative power of the states in which they hold citizenship" (2004, 42). Yet I also want to complicate this assertion by underscoring the ways in which citizens who come from poor countries, those from both urban and rural backgrounds, may have "middle-class income that can afford them meals out, maids, entertainment, and other luxuries that are far more expensive, and difficult to come by in the United States, Western Europe, or Japan" (Constable 2005, 10–11). In the same way, Mayfair Yang has critically pointed out that the rise of cosmopolitanism in the homeland frequently means that "those who have stayed in the country have started to undergo a change in subjectivity that is perhaps just as dramatic as that of those who have traveled abroad" (1997, 311).

This book explains how and why international marriages allow individuals in the context of globalization and transnational networks "to consider a wider set of 'possible' lives than they ever did before" (Appadurai 1991, 197). My findings dispel two specific popular discourses about contemporary international marriage markets—the simplistic ideas that men from rich countries go to poor ones for submissive wives, and that women from poor countries go to rich ones for husbands who will provide economically for them. Throughout this book, I show how international marriages in the Vietnamese diaspora provide an important example of how economic activities and intimacies sustain each other, and that it would be difficult to understand, as noted by Viviana Zelizer, the coexistence of the economy and intimacy "if you think that economic self-interest determines all social relations, if you imagine that the world splits sharply into separate spheres of rationality and sentiment, or if you suppose that intimacy is a delicate plant that can only survive in a thick-windowed greenhouse" (2005, 2). The case studies I present show how "love and emotion are intertwined with political economy through cultural logics of desire" (Constable 2003, 119). It would be improper, I contend, to understand macrostructural forces such as globalization and transnationalism simply through material analysis offered by dominant political-economic approaches. This is because simply "reducing an individual's life-altering decisions to seemingly 'rational' calculations fails to recognize the humanity and sentiment of even the most ruthless and seemingly pragmatic acts" (ibid., 119–120).

As one scholar argues, "motivational-only" theories of migration may only partly explain why people want to migrate, but cannot explain why they are able to do so (Yang 1995). In other words, individuals need to have migration resources such as networks and kin to carry out the move from one country to another, and to overcome legal, financial, and administrative barriers. On the other hand, scholars who focus on migration resources, such as immigrants' social networks (Massey, Alarcon, Durand, and Gonzalez 1987), as the determining factor in deciding the size and direction of migration flows, tend to ignore personal motivations. Social networks may explain how individuals are able to migrate, but cannot explain why they want to do so. Both motivation and resources are important factors to help explain international marriage migration patterns. But the scholarly literature often frames both dimensions in economic terms, thereby impeding our understanding of subjective experiences in globalization. The impetus for this book, for that reason, lies in the argument that marital decisions across international borders must take into account a fundamental and critical missing element in current analysis of globalization, what anthropologist Caroline Brettell (2006) calls the "symbolic, affective, and psychosocial" dimensions of transnationalism. I view the pages that follow as an exploratory look at how international marriages bring forth questions of emotional belonging across transnational space. Such questions, if placed in a diasporic context, as Lok Siu observes, are part of "an ongoing formation of a consciousness, a positioning, a subjective expression of living at the intersection of different cultural-national formations" (2005, 4).

I must note at the outset that in recent years, important studies have documented various types of international marriages, including the situations of interracial and interethnic marriages within and outside of Asia (Kelsky 2001; Suzuki 2003), commercialized international marriages among internet mail-order brides (Constable 2003; Schaeffer-Grabiel 2004), traditional systems of commercialized marriage brokering (Wang and Chang 2003), military brides (Yuh 2002), transnational arranged marriages among South Asian diasporic subjects living in Europe (Balzani 2006; Charsley 2005, 2006; Charsley and Shaw 2006), and marriages among sex workers and their clients (Brennan 2004; Kempadoo 2004). The present study adds to this ongoing effort by offering the first book-length study since the post-1965 immigration era that specifically highlights international marriages among individuals of the same ethnicity living in different parts of the world. I seek to underscore social meanings and processes embedded in international marriages that will assist us in understanding the material reality and cultural struggles of what Raymond Williams (1972) calls a "structure of feeling," a consciousness derived from actively lived and felt relationships. At the heart of the matter is that contemporary international marriages in the Vietnamese diaspora allow us to call attention to the legacy of war in this part of the world, which produced initial migratory paths that consequently, and in multiple ways, necessitated these international marriages.

ACKNOWLEDGMENTS

THIS BOOK REQUIRED more time, money, movements, and emotions than I had ever imagined it would cost me. First, I am grateful to the transpacific husbands and wives and their families who shared the stories of their lives with me. From the transpacific husbands in this study, I learned about the significance of "home," and from the transpacific wives, I learned about the significance of wanting to go away. I suspect some of my informants—both men and women—may ultimately disagree with my analysis, and may even contest how I represent their lives. But I have written this book with their struggles and hardships in mind. I regret that they must remain anonymous.

At Rutgers University Press, I am grateful to my acquisitions editor, Kristi Long, for her initial ideas on the project, and then to my book editor, Adi Hovav, who provided comments and feedback that made the book more readable. Adi is a first-rate editor with a special eye for understanding readers' needs. I am indebted to Margaret Case for her meticulous work on copyediting the book, and to Marilyn Campbell and her staff for their work on all the details during the production.

My greatest debt, which I can never truly return, is to Barrie Thorne, who believed in me and encouraged me to move along each and every step of the way during the entire time that it took me to write this book. She is the best role model for a scholar and teacher, a wonderful friend, and truly a great human being. Intellectually, Barrie guided my sociological imagination, always allowing me to choose my own intellectual tastes and styles. She has always been there to listen when I had anything to say, and always offered to assist me in my journey into the academy and, in many ways, through life. Barrie has read many drafts of this book. She wrote countless letters for fellowships and grants, and supported my intellectual taste even when she disagreed with it. I hope that I can repay her one day.

Arlie Russell Hochschild has an amazing skill for asking questions and thinking about small things that constitute social forces. I will be forever grateful for the intellectual tools she has given me, especially her constant push to make sociology accessible to the public. I benefited a great deal from her skills as an interviewer and a listener, from her approach to the academic enterprise, and from her sensibility to research respondents. Evelyn Nakano Glenn and Peter Zinoman asked some difficult questions that made the project better. I am thankful that they believed in the project and hope this book will meet some of their expectations. Among my list of educators, one other person must be thanked. When I was an undergraduate at the University of Florida, I dared to take a women's studies course and found myself in a class of fifty students as the only man and only person of color. I thought about immediately dropping the course, but the professor, Mary Ann Leiby, encouraged me to stay. That is how I became seriously interested in issues of gender and inequality.

The research for this book was costly, as I had to travel back and forth between Vietnam and the United States, and to undertake research trips to four metropolitan areas in the United States. Several institutions and organizations gave a total of over twenty grants and fellowships that made all that possible. I am indebted to the Social Science Research Council in New York City for a grant that allowed me to take a trip to Vietnam in the summer of 1999. The SSRC also facilitated an Immigration Workshop that helped to move the project along. I especially want to acknowledge the support of George Sanchez, who directed that summer workshop in Irvine, and to the group of scholars who were part of the workshop, especially Yen Le Espiritu, Min Zhou, and Pierrette Hondagneu-Sotelo, who helped me think through the research design in the very early phases of this research. I received a fellowship from the Hewlett Foundation that allowed me to undertake eight months of fieldwork in Vietnam. At Berkeley, I received grants from the Berkeley Sociology Department, minigrants from the Berkeley Sigmi-Xi Honor Society, as well as generous funding from the Berkeley Humanities Research Program. The Berkeley Vice Chancellor for Research grant, which came along at just the right time, allowed me to do the interviews with transpacific husbands in Seattle, Boston, Los Angeles, and San Francisco. In Santa Barbara, I received generous grants that allowed me to take time off from teaching. These included faculty research grants from the Institute for Social, Behavioral, and Economics Research, the Interdisciplinary Humanities Center, the Junior Faculty Research Incentives Program, the Academic Senate, and the University of California Regents' Faculty Fellowship Program.

I am indebted to my colleagues in the Asian American Studies Department for providing an intellectually vibrant and congenial environment. Celine Parrenas Shimizu provided intellectual support and great fun. I owe her a lot for enhancing my experience while in Santa Barbara. Arlene Phillips came on the scene when I was a new faculty member and did everything to make my life easier on the administrative front. When she found out that I decided to quit smoking after I finished one of the first versions of this book, Arlene appeared at my office one day with a huge bag of Starburst candy. She is a first-rate departmental manager, and I appreciate her more than she probably realizes. Two people in Santa Barbara require special mention. I thank Sarah Fenstermaker for supporting and listening to all my problems during my first year as an assistant professor and for helping me navigate the world of UCSB. Her visit to me in

Vietnam is unforgettable. Ingrid Banks provided much needed support and laughter, for which I am indebted.

I would like to acknowledge Dr. Nghia The Nguyen for facilitating my ties to the Institute for Social Sciences in Ho Chi Minh City and to Professor Kim Xuyen Thi Tran for facilitating my involvement with the Sociology Department at the University of Humanities and Social Sciences in Ho Chi Minh City. For research assistance, I owe a great deal to Sang, who is the world's best motorcyclist. In Vietnam, Sang took me to most of the interviews I conducted, and he provided enormous insights into contemporary Vietnam. He was an amazing research assistant and a wonderful friend, making sure that my research went smoothly. Xuan Hanh Thi Nguyen, Nga Thi Nguyen, and Loc Mai Huu provided research assistance in Vietnam for which I am very grateful. In the United States, I am indebted to my student research assistants, including Linh Nguyen, Hang Nguyen, Christal Pham, Lily Ngoc, Diana Olin, Niki Runge, Ciera Divens, Kyla Johnson, and Laura Enriquez. Linh helped to transcribe over half of the interviews, and Hang helped me with translating the initial project proposal into Vietnamese so that I could gain affiliation with the Institute for Social Sciences in Vietnam. In the last stage of this project, Laura Enriquez helped with analysis and linguistic mistakes. She is a first-rate and very humorous editor.

I am incredibly privileged to be back to Pomona College in Claremont, California, where I was a scholar-in-residence before heading off to UCSB as an assistant professor. My decision to return to Pomona College reflects how special this liberal arts college is to me. It is a wonderful community of intellectual vibrancy among students and faculty. When I was a scholar-in-residence while in my last year of graduate school, Pomona College provided extremely generous funding and an academic paradise during much of the writing stage of this project. I owe a great deal to Pat Smiley, who was then associate dean, and to

Dean Gary Kates for providing funding so that I could take my entire class on "transnational families" to Vietnam in 2002 on a field trip to learn about families of transmigrants. I owe a great deal to those twelve students who went to Vietnam with me. They provided feedback on ideas, as well as being wonderfully engaged with the materials I taught them.

In Claremont, I am fortunate to have wonderful colleagues at the college, especially in the Intercollegiate Department of Asian American Studies and in the Department of Sociology. I thank Samuel Hideo Yamashita, Sharon Goto, David Elliott, Duong Van Mai Elliott, Lynne Miyake, Linus Yamane, David Yoo, You Young Kang, Thomas Kim, Ming-Yuen Ma, Seung Hye Suh, Kathy Yep, Jill Grigsby, Robert Herman, Lynn Rapaport, Gilda Ochoa, and Sheila Pinkel. The many spontaneous conversations in the hallways of Hanh, Mead, and Lincoln and our collective efforts in cultivating the wonderful young minds at Pomona College constantly remind me why I chose a life in the academy. I especially thank Gilda and Jill for reading parts of the manuscript and giving important feedback that sharpened the arguments. Right from the beginning of my return to Pomona College, Jill has welcomed me in every way and has gone out of her way as a mentor and a friend. Jill is a role model in numerous ways, and I look forward to many more laughs and spontaneous conversations. I owe enormous gratitude to Gail Orozco, who is the most patient departmental manager in the universe, for making life in the Hanh building a wonderful one. Of course, all of my experiences at Pomona College would not be possible without Lynn Rapaport, who initially organized and facilitated my presence at Pomona College as a scholar-in-residence, and who, as former chair of the Department of Sociology, helped to make it possible for my return to the college.

I am fortunate to have four dear friends who understand my life goals in ways that few people can. Ajay Deshmukh, Anil

Reddy, and Sergey Ioffe made the Berkeley years fun. Without them, I would have been very lonely, and the Berkeley years, without doubt, would have been very incomplete. They are great models of the "new men" in this country, who value egalitarianism and frequently challenge hegemonic notions of masculinity. And Jinnhua Su is truly the "childhood friend" of my adult life. He constantly reminds me, even if he does not know it, of how important it is just to have fun. I thank him for forcing me to take the first trip to Brazil with him at a moment's notice. Jinnhua is a first-rate lawyer, but he is also a sociologist at heart whose ideas have helped me think deeply about my work and people's everyday struggle for respect.

Jane Zavisca listened and gave wonderful support in the form of conversations and companionship. I will always remember our trip to Russia and our experiences with the Vietnamese communities in Moscow and St. Petersburg. Robyn Rodriguez gave enormous support from the beginning of graduate school. She inspired me to visit the Philippines and the refugee camp where my family lived when I was a child. My friends in different parts of the world, including William Golden, Julie Todd, Chanh Van Phan, Ha Ta, Patrick Froehlich, Alex Holleitner, Debbie Holleitner, Nhan Nguyen, Thuy Diep Thi Duong, Thuc Nguyen, and Zion Mitchell remind me that friendships can endure despite long distances over many years.

My father, Hoang Van Thai, gave every support along the way, including the little money that he had. My mother, Pham Thi Lien, tragically passed away a month before I finished the first version of this book. I knew my mother very briefly, having been reunited with her in my early twenties after being separated when I was three. She is the very reason why I did this project, so that I could make my way "home" to be with her for that one year while doing fieldwork. She taught me about the need to take pleasures and luxuries in life. My eldest sister Thi helped me to realize the significance of Vietnam as a place in our lives, and she, having endured the most difficult and unfair childhood of anyone I know, is the most influential and resilient person in my life. The world would be a better place if everyone was lucky enough to have a sister like her. My nephew Nicholas Nguyen lived with me in Santa Barbara when he was nine years old, the year I wrote half of this book. My only regret was that my work was a distraction to our wonderful time together. I owe him so much for constantly reminding me that my work "is not that important, Uncle number four." I will truly cherish the year he lived with me.

A Note on Translations

Vietnamese is a tonal language with varying regional dialects that requires the use of complex diacritic marks. Following other researchers (Luong 1992; Malarney 1996; Marr 1981, 1997; Rydstrom 2003; Zinoman 2001), I have chosen to not employ diacritic marks in order to facilitate smooth reading. In addition, as with any research involving translations, some words do not have exact translations into the English language, and some words lose their complexity once translated. When translations seriously lose intended meanings, I have provided Vietnamese translations in parentheses without diacritic marks.

For Better or For Worse

Marriage and Migration in the New Global Economy

INTERNATIONAL MARRIAGE is currently the primary reason why people migrate to the United States (Rumbaut 1997; United States Department of Homeland Security 2006; USINS 2002). As figure 1.1 illustrates, of all the immigrants entering the United States in 2005, 58 percent came through various routes of family sponsorship.[1] Of all family-sponsored immigrants, as shown in figure 1.2, the largest single mode of sponsorship was marriage with either a U.S. citizen or a permanent resident. Nearly half of all family-sponsored immigrants arrived as international marriage migrants in 2005.[2] These marriage migrants constituted over a quarter of all the immigrants who entered, almost triple the proportion (a mere 9 percent) of marriage migrants who came to the United States in the 1960s. Women make up more than 65 percent of all marriage migrants. Whereas marriage migrants make up about a quarter of all men who enter the United States each year, female marriage migrants constitute over 40 percent of all women who enter. Furthermore, individuals of the same ethnicity currently constitute an estimated two-thirds of all marriage migration couples (United States Department of Homeland Security 2006; USINS 1999a; USINS 1999b).

Although international marriages and other family-related factors explain why the majority of contemporary migrants come to the United States each year, few have studied that side

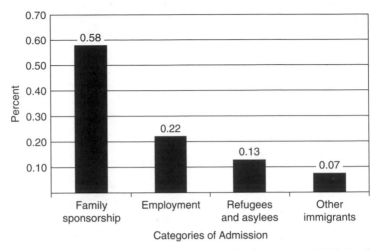

1-1. Percent of Immigrants by Categories of Admission in 2005 Total Number of Immigrants: 1,122,373 Source: U.S. Department of Homeland Security, *Yearbook of Immigration Statistics*, 2005, table 7.

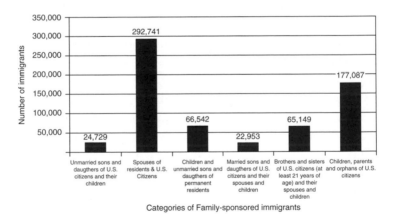

1-2. Family-Sponsored Immigrants in 2005 (Total = 649,2001) Source: U.S. Department of Homeland Security, *Yearbook of Immigration Statistics*, 2005, table 7.

of immigration. Issues of poverty, war, the search for jobs, and political asylum tend to dominate the field of contemporary migration studies. Consequently, we know very little about the dynamics of different contemporary international marriage migration streams, why it is that women are overwhelmingly the sponsored spouse, and why it is that immigrants are increasingly turning to their home countries for marriage partners.

What we do know, or think we know, about marriage migration frequently focuses on extremely dichotomous images of women as either the "helpless victims of controlling U.S. men" or as scheming agents, "shrewd foreigners out for a green card and a free meal ticket through marriage fraud and immigration scams that dupe innocent U.S. men" (Constable 2003, 13). Indeed, marriage choice in the West is frequently thought of in simplistic "either or" terms. That is to say, people are thought to marry to form an economic partnership, thus for material needs, or they marry for love, sex, and romance to fulfill emotional needs (Kalmijn 1998). This bipolar view is, of course, highly problematic in the context of international and immigration communities. I aim to complicate this picture so as to provide a more nuanced portrait of the ways in which economic activities and intimate relations are, in numerous ways, forged and sustained by each other in the contemporary global arena. Like Constable, I argue against a "dichotomous or discontinuous view of love and opportunism that treats pragmatic concerns as incompatible with emotional ones" (ibid., 11). In this way, I join dialogues raised by feminist ethnographers in recent times who have shifted away from simple hierarchies and dichotomies to more nuanced "problematization of multiple spaces, seemingly contradictory social locations and plural sites of power" (Kempadoo 1999, 234).

THE MARRIAGE MARKETS OF THE VIETNAMESE DIASPORA

The Vietnamese diaspora provides one distinct example of international marriages in the new global economy among individuals of the same ethnicity living in different parts of the world. Through various routes of passage over the past three decades, over two million people have emigrated from Vietnam. They represent the core group of refugees who have fled Southeast Asia since the withdrawal of American troops from Vietnam and the fall of Saigon on April 30, 1975. Approximately 60 percent left as boat refugees; the remaining 40 percent went directly to resettlement countries. Of all these emigrants, 94 percent eventually resettled in Western countries, mostly in the United States, Canada, Australia, and France.[3] In the United States, the Vietnamese emerged as an entirely new, yet immediately visible, ethnic group just over thirty years ago. Before 1950, according to the United States Immigration and Naturalization Service (USINS 2002), there were only a few more than 300 Vietnamese in the United States. And before 1975, there were fewer than 18,000.[4] Most of these pre-1975 migrants came as either students, wives of U.S. servicemen, or trainees on non-immigrant visas (Skinner 1980). Since 1975, the Vietnamese have constituted America's single largest group of refugees, and Vietnam remains one of the top five countries with the highest rates of emigration to the United States (United States Department of Homeland Security 2006). Their experiences of migration, often framed in vocabularies of exile and displacement, have been the focus of considerable research by scholars and journalists over the last three decades.[5]

One important, yet understudied, manifestation of Vietnamese out-migration in the last quarter of the twentieth century is that single people across the Vietnamese diaspora are pressed by what demographer Daniel Goodkind (1997) calls the "Vietnamese double marriage squeeze," which is a peculiar, if not unique, situation in the worldwide marriage market for any ethnic or cultural group. A shortage of one sex or the other in the age group in which marriage generally occurs is often termed a marriage squeeze (Guttentag and Secord 1983). The Vietnamese double marriage squeeze specifically refers to the low ratio of males to females in Vietnam and the unusually high ratio of males to females in the Vietnamese diaspora. A high male mortality rate during the Vietnam War, combined with the migration of a larger number of men than women during the past quarter of the twentieth century, has produced a low ratio of men to women in Vietnam, along with an unusually high ratio of men to women in the Vietnamese diaspora, especially in Australia and in the United States. Of the fifteen most populous nations in 1989, for instance, Vietnam had the lowest ratio of men to women at the peak marrying ages. By 1999, there were approximately 92 men for every 100 women between the ages of 30 and 34 in Vietnam. The reverse situation prevails in the diaspora: in 2000, there were 129 Vietnamese-American men for every 100 women between the ages of 24 and 29. Among Vietnamese Americans aged 30 to 34, there were about 135 for every 100 women.[6]

Sex-ratio imbalances are important to consider because they help to explain, in the words of Yen Le Espiritu, "the importance of immigration policies in shaping the demographic context within which immigrant men and women have to interact" (1997, 9). Previous research points to sex-ratio imbalances as a key structural condition that drove co-ethnic international marriages in the early periods of Asian immigration to the United States. The dominant explanation, best articulated by scholars such as Sucheng Chan (1991), Evelyn Nakano Glenn (1986), and Yen Le Espiritu (1997), is that racist immigration policies and gendered labor recruitment practices from the mid-nineteenth to the early twentieth centuries restricted the immigration of women from Asia, resulting in severe sex-ratio imbalances among early Asian immigrants, who consequently faced tremendous challenges to form or maintain families across national borders. Racist exclusionary policies, starting with the Page Law of 1875, which led to the Chinese Exclusion Act of 1882 and then eventually the National Origins Act of 1924, restricted the ability of Asian immigrant men to sponsor wives into the United States.[7] To appreciate the magnitude of feminized exclusion policies, consider that fifteen years after the enactment of the Page Law, the sex ratio among Chinese Americans was at 27 men for every woman.[8] Similarly unbalanced sex ratios were also experienced by the Japanese, Filipinos, Koreans, and Indians.[9]

Racist immigration policies that excluded women in the early decades of Asian American immigration produced few options for family formation like those that were afforded to European immigrants during the same period. Among Europeans, married men often migrated first and later easily sent for their wives and children, while single men were able to find marital partners among subsequent flows of single women who migrated, often for the sole purpose of finding husbands, as Suzanne Sinke has documented (1999; Sinke and Gross 1992). Once they were familiar with the United States, some European single men could easily return to their country of origin to marry and later have their wives migrate. In contrast, Asian American men were not able to return to Asia for wives because the passage was too expensive for them, because they feared they could not return to the United States once they left, or because they were afraid of being drafted in their country's military (Chan 1991).

The Asian American marriage squeeze for men was amplified by that fact that until the mid-twentieth century, bachelors were not allowed to marry white women legally, although as Chan (1991) points out, miscegenation laws did not really affect Asians since many early Asian immigrants did not want to outmarry in the first place. Thus, racial discrimination in immigration policies and gendered labor recruitment practices resulting in severe sex-ratio skews best explain why Asian American men of the past returned to or sent for brides from their home countries. Likewise, given the dramatic shortage of marriageable women in the contemporary Vietnamese diaspora and, to a lesser extent, the shortage of marriageable men in Vietnam, contemporary immigrant Vietnamese men have a compelling reason for returning to their home country for wives. But while the numbers are significant, I suggest that they tell only part of the story for contemporary international marriages in the Vietnamese diaspora.

MARITAL SUBJECTIVITIES
IN GLOBAL SPACE

My inquiry into contemporary international marriages is heavily informed by the groundbreaking work in transnational migration scholarship that was inaugurated in the United States in the 1990s, growing out of a sturdy critique of the assimilationist paradigm that began with the so-called Chicago School in the 1920s. This assimilationist approach, which dominated the literature on immigrants and immigration from the 1920s until the early 1990s, paid attention to the incorporation of new immigrants and to "domestic attempts at managing the influx of refugees, migrant workers, and foreign capital on the social and political body of the nation" (Ong 1999, 8). In this version of immigration theories, competing explanations point to the nature of the "world system" that exploits those from peripheral countries, or to the "push and pull" factors embedded in global unequal development that compel individual migrants to move across national borders for better life opportunities. These competing immigration theories form the basic foundation for the new theoretical articulations in the field of transnational migration studies. There are some excellent recent assessments of the field's efforts.[10] Here, however, I raise the point that, despite some important movement toward bringing a gender analysis to transnational migration scholarship, there is still a marked lack of attention to the role of men and masculinity and, more important, to the ways that gender operates on the most interpersonal level across transnational social space (Curran et al. 2006; Donato et al. 2006; Mahler and Pessar 2006; Pessar and Mahler 2003).

GENDER AND TRANSNATIONAL
MIGRATION

A brief assessment of research in the field reveals that there is a chronological paradox in research on gender and transmigration. From the 1950s to the 1970s, scholarship on migration focused almost exclusively on men as the "birds of passage," while women, children, and the elderly were seen as following in their paths (Bodnar, Simon, and Weber 1982; Handlin 1951; Howe 1976; Piore 1979; Brettell and Simon 1986). This earlier research assumed that males were more inclined and able to take risks and to journey far away in search of better job opportunities, whereas women, if they migrated at all, were depicted as emotional caretakers who accompanied men to ensure family and community stability. In the 1970s and 1980s, scholars began to focus on women as central actors in the migration process, in part because of the dramatic growth in feminist scholarship and women's studies programs as well as demographic reports showing that more women than men were migrating to the United States (Houstoun, Kramer, and Barrett 1984). During the 1990s, a lively body of literature that treated gender as a central theoretical concept in migration patterns was added to the few previous works.[11]

But while there have been enormous efforts to bring women into the picture on migration, the comparative immigration circumstances of men to women have been relatively neglected in the past three decades. Thus, the paradox of contemporary research on gender and migration is that while women became a central concern over the past three decades, the situations of men have been left out, thereby impeding our understanding of gender relations and gendered processes in migration flows. As pointed out by two prominent scholars on gender and transmigration, "many scholars write that they are studying 'gender,' yet examine only women," and "there was a time when the exclusive male-only focus needed this corrective but we feel that this time has passed" (Mahler and Pessar 2006,

50–51). The dominant prevailing view of gender in current research is that, as Robert Courtney Smith explains, first-generation men "are seen to want to return home or to imagine themselves returning, whereas women want to settle or imagine themselves settling, because men lose status and power in the United States and women gain them" (2006, 13).

The analysis presented in this book moves beyond this dominant approach into what Pierrette Hondagneu-Sotelo calls the current "third" stage of gender and migration research that examines the "extent to which gender permeates a variety of practices, identities, and institutions implicated in immigration . . . in ways that reveal how gender is incorporated into a myriad of daily operations and institutional political and economic structures" (2003, 9). By raising the issue of masculinity as it relates to gender dynamics in the discussions on globalization and transnationalism, I join the dialogue raised by feminist theorists who have engaged in demonstrating that gender plays a key role in the constitution and formation of national subjectivities and collectivities (Abu-Lughod 1998; Alonso 1994; Chatterjee 1993; Espiritu 1997; Lowe 1996). I see many processes occurring in what Sarah Mahler and Patricia Pessar call "gendered geographies of power," a framework that helps us understand "people's social agency—corporal and cognitive—given their own initiative as well as their positioning within multiple hierarchies of power operative within and across many terrains" (2001, 447). Mahler and Pessar suggest that power struggles in transnational space involve not only spatial scales but also social scales, both of which produce social locations that explain a person's "positions within power hierarchies created through historical, political, economic, geographic, kinship-based, and other socially stratifying factors" (ibid., 445–446).

SOCIAL FIELDS OF WORTH

Moving away from simply documenting "systems of oppression" at work in gendered transnational processes (Brennan 2004, 24),

I take up the question of convertibility of social worth and respect evinced by a specific diasporic group as they produce and interpret symbolic, affective, and psychosocial dynamics in processes of international marriage migration. What is primarily at issue here is the nature of how and why individuals are able to convert certain forms of capital across transnational space in order to achieve social worth and respect as they make decisions about international marriage and international migration. The analysis I present in the chapters that follow is inspired by Pierre Bourdieu's theory of social fields (1977, 1980, 1984, 1989; Bourdieu and Wacquant 1992). In Bourdieu's view, a social field is an arena where social struggles and social achievements take place and the contests are over access to specific forms of capital, as well as the ability or inability to convert a specific capital from one form to another. In any social field, social positions are assigned a certain level of worth, and a field will have a specific structural context for producing interests and strategies to accumulate and convert capital. It is, in Bourdieu's words, "a configuration of objective relations between positions objectively defined, in their existence and in the determinations they impose upon their occupants, agents or institutions, by their present and potential situation . . . in the structure of the distribution of power (or capital) whose possession commands access to the specific profits that are at stake in the field, as well as by their objective relation to other positions" (1989, 39).

Social fields are microcosms where the convertibility of various forms of capital is possible from one field to another while, at the same time, "a capital does not exist and function but in relation to a field" (Wacquant 1989, 39). In other words, the value of capital is meaningless if it is not constituted by or attached to a specific social field. The concept of social field is crucial to our understanding of conversion of certain kinds of capital for another because it explicitly recognizes that different forms of capital are valued or devalued according to which social field they belong. The potential shifting of value in capital across social fields mandates that we think about social struggles, since individuals will strategize to preserve their capital or undermine others in their field. As Bourdieu explains:

> As a space of potential and active forces, the field is also a *field of struggle* aimed at preserving or transforming the configurations of these forces. Concretely, the field as a structure of objective relations of force between positions undergirds and guides the strategies whereby the occupants of these positions seek, individually or collectively, to safeguard or improve their position, and to impose the principle of hierarchization most favorable to their own products. The strategies of agents depend on their position in the field, that is, in the distribution of the specific field. (Wacquant 1989, 40)

In a field of struggle, therefore, social worth is based not only on economic capital (income, for example) but is linked to other forms of capital, namely, cultural, social, and symbolic. Distinctions using any form of capital exist in social fields, because differentiations are made by individuals and social groups in order to legitimate symbolic or material power. Social fields are, in short, sites of conflict. It is this site of conflict, I contend, that scholars of globalization and transnationalism may find most interesting and problematic in Bourdieu's theory of convertibility and social fields. This is because one of the most important critiques of Bourdieu is the question of convertibility across international boundaries, since for Bourdieu, differences are marked within specific "objective social space" (Hall 1992, 279). Thus, while Bourdieu's approach, as Nina Glick Schiller notes, "does not preclude the notion of transnational social fields, he does not directly discuss the implications of social fields that are not coterminous with state boundaries" (2005, 442). What kinds of capital are convertible across transnational social fields in processes of international marriage? How and why does the process of international convertibility bring social worth in marital choice? Why is the process of convertibility gendered?

GETTING TO KNOW MARRIED PEOPLE ACROSS TRANSNATIONAL SOCIAL FIELDS

During fourteen months of fieldwork done in distinct intervals in Vietnam and in the United States between June 1997 and March 2001, I got to know 129 individuals, including brides, grooms, and their family members, who were involved in a total of 69 Vietnamese international marriages. The complicated process of doing fieldwork in two countries requires a lengthy discussion in order to situate the case studies of specific marriages in the chapters to follow. To begin this discussion, it is important first to understand that in this distinct and emergent global marriage market, immigrant Vietnamese men typically go to Vietnam to marry through arrangement by kin networks, and subsequently return to their places of residence in the Vietnamese diaspora to initiate paperwork to sponsor their wives as immigrants, while the wives wait in Vietnam for the paperwork to clear. The couples I got to know in these marriages were, therefore, in this "migration waiting period." That is, they were transnationally separated as the women were waiting to unite with their husbands through migration.

During this waiting period, I came to know them by first entering the lives of the brides in Vietnam and later the U.S.-based grooms. For the most part, because I strategically did not interview international couples—wives *and* husbands—while they were in one place, I am providing an analysis about a specific period of time, a "snapshot" of marriage and migration during the waiting period. The data analysis presented here accordingly centers on peoples' thoughts, emotions, motives, and expectations about marriage prior to taking up shared residence, and about migration as couples were waiting to physically unite. Since most of the couples had not known each other for long prior to marriage, they were just beginning to form opinions and expectations about each other and about what marriage might mean to them in local and projected future contexts.

After the initial trip to Vietnam in the summer of 1997 that I discussed in the preface, I subsequently embarked on an intensive stint of fieldwork for eight months in Vietnam beginning in December 1999, followed by three months in the United States beginning in January 2001.[12] During the first trip to Vietnam, I made initial connections with officials at the Institute for Social Sciences in Ho Chi Minh City, hereafter referred to as the Institute, who assisted me in gathering the required permission from the Vietnamese government to conduct the study in Saigon and in the Mekong Delta. These two areas represented a large portion of southern Vietnam, which was a good strategic starting point for studying the Vietnamese diaspora because of its history of out-migration. Scholars of Vietnam have long noted the relevance of taking a regional approach to study this country, since different regions have varied patterns of marriage, household composition, and family relations (Belanger 2000; Belanger and Hong 1996; Goodkind 1997; Hirschman and Loi 1996; Rambo 1973). The south in general has a long history of out-migration to the West after and because of the Vietnam War. At the time that I began the research, only ten years after the inauguration of the *Doi Moi* economic reform, industrial parks on the outskirts of Saigon and in rice paddies of the nearby Mekong Delta produced two-thirds of the nation's wealth, accounting for 80 percent of its tax revenue (Pierre 2000). At least eleven large-scale condominium-style apartments and numerous villa-style homes, catering exclusively to the Viet Kieu community, were being built in and around Saigon while I did fieldwork.

INITIAL PLANS

When I began the first long period of fieldwork in 1999, I initially planned to recruit respondents through snowball sampling, a technique in which researchers begin from a core of known informants and then increase the sample by adding new informants referred by members of the initial core (Glaser and Strauss 1967; Gubrium 1990; Weiss 1995). The first problem I faced with fieldwork using this sampling strategy surfaced early on, because officials at the Institute said that in order to acquire permission to conduct my fieldwork, I needed to devise probability sampling procedures by obtaining names of couples from marriage registration lists. This was when I came to understand that in order to initiate migration paperwork for sponsoring the wives' migration to join their husbands overseas, Vietnamese international couples had to first register their marriages in a special unit for "Viet Kieu marriages" at the Vietnamese Department of Justice (So Tu Phap). The Institute wanted me to extract a probability sample by obtaining names of couples who registered their marriages, instead of using snowball sampling through my social networks.[13]

Once I agreed to obtain a probability sample, I received full permission to conduct fieldwork with the stipulation that I was assigned a research assistant, whom I shall call Sang, who was required to accompany me at every *first* interview with informants in Vietnam. One of the first things Sang did for me was to accompany me to the Department of Justice in Saigon and in a rural province in the Mekong Delta that I call Se Long, located about 135 miles southwest of Saigon, to obtain names of registered married people.[14] We received two lists of names of registered marriages, 200 names of couples from Saigon and 120 names of couples from Se Long.

THE REGISTERED MARRIAGES

It is important to note that the lists of names of couples we received were recently registered marriages, not recently married couples, although most were, in fact, recently married.[15] The two lists of registered marriages included grooms who came from over thirty countries and sixteen states in the United States, but in my sampling procedures, the brides in this sample married grooms who were living in eight different countries (the United States, Australia, Canada, France, England, Belgium, Norway, and Germany).[16] I was able to interview brides who married grooms from all over the diaspora, since the brides were still residing in Vietnam. Given financial limitations, however, I was only able to interview U.S.-based grooms. The project, therefore, was divided into two phases of research during the migration waiting period: a "bride phase" in Vietnam and a "groom phase" in the United States. During this waiting period, I came to know international couples by first entering the lives of the brides in Vietnam and subsequently the U.S.-based grooms in the four metropolitan areas of Los Angeles, San Francisco, Seattle, and Boston.[17]

Readers interested in the technical details of the sampling procedures can consult appendix A, but here, I note that the final analysis is based on a sample of 69 marriages, the unit of analysis in this study. In the bride phase in Vietnam, I conducted multiple formal tape-recorded in-depth interviews with 93 individuals, including brides and their family members.[18] In the groom phase in the United States, I interviewed 36 individuals, including grooms and their family members.[19] In other words, in some of these marriages I did not necessarily interview the grooms, and in a few marriages I did not interview the brides, but frequently interviews with their family members provided sufficient information on a marriage that I included such marriages in my sample. In total I conducted 181 tape-recorded interviews with 129 individuals across the Vietnamese diaspora.[20]

In addition to formal tape-recorded in-depth interviews with the wives and their families in Vietnam, I chose eight families in Saigon, on the basis of a variety of considerations such as age, level of education, income, and contexts of transnational networks, and asked them to allow me to enter their homes for participant observation.[21] These families allowed me to visit their homes and to follow them (e.g., to the market, migration offices, and family rituals) as they conducted their daily lives.[22] To further understand the lives of single adults who might enter the marriage market in Vietnam, I regularly attended dance clubs, bars, and health clubs that catered, sometimes exclusively, to overseas Vietnamese men in Saigon and local women in Vietnam. I also attended cooking classes for local women at the Saigonese Women's Union, since I had heard that many women take cooking classes in preparation for marriage. Through this process, I found out that people were not meeting each other in public spaces, and why not, as I discuss in chapter 6.

TRANSNATIONAL SPLIT HOUSEHOLDS AND FAKE MARRIAGES

I encountered two issues that deserve mentioning. First, 12 percent (n = 8/69) of the couples in this sample did not choose to register their marriages immediately after they were married because the wives did not intend to go abroad; the couple thus intended to maintain a transnational split household indefinitely. Three of the couples told me that they maintained transnational split households because the husbands encountered difficulties sponsoring the wives abroad, while other husbands found it more affordable to have their wives in Vietnam because it was cheaper to support them there with remittances than to have the wives migrate overseas—a pattern also true in historical cases of international marriages in Asian America (Chan 1991). Eventually, however, when migration was or became the goal, the couples registered their marriages, and that was how they got into my sample of registered marriages, even though some of these couples had been married for a long time.[23]

The other issue I encountered was fake marriages. For the process of marriage registration, grooms and brides needed to verify their status as single people and that they were disease-free. Medical exam proved their health, and women obtained papers verifying their single status from their local police. Men living overseas, however, verified their single status by obtaining papers at local courthouses in their overseas contexts. When I found out about the requirement to verify single status, several questions arose. Had some of these men married overseas, but perhaps never filed marriage certificates? Perhaps some of them returned to Vietnam for a second wife or for a mistress, as some people in Vietnam thought. And were there single men who were paid by wealthy women to take part in fake marriages so that they could migrate abroad?

I did, in fact, encounter some people outside of my sample who participated in fake marriages. Some men duped local women, but some women duped the overseas men, too, for visas. Some men went as far as to have elaborate and expensive weddings and have sex with their virgin wives, only to leave the women once they returned to their overseas contexts. On the other hand, some women married overseas men, but once they obtained their visas to go abroad, their husbands never heard from them. I also met wealthy women who paid overseas men, usually between US$20,000 and $30,000, to sponsor them overseas through fake international marriages. Taking account of these possibilities of fake and duped marriages, I explicitly asked the brides to not participate in my study if they were in fake marriages or if their husbands were currently married to another woman abroad. I believe, though I can never be sure, that this request eliminated those possibilities. This was a difficult choice to make, and was an issue I thought about during each interview I conducted, since I suppose some feared that if they did not participate in my study, I would suspect that they were, in fact, in fake marriages. I was worried about this because I thought some of the couples might have thought that I worked for the embassy, who could decide on the issuance of their visas to migrate abroad.[24] Although these sorts of variations could possibly be part of my data, I am not attempting to capture these unusual experiences in this book, which is perhaps one limitation of this study. Rather, my goal is to understand how individuals across the Vietnamese diaspora make decisions about international marriages, reflect on their marriageability across time, and define their expectations for such marriages as they eagerly wait to unite across time and space.

OVERVIEW OF THE BOOK

This study is unusual in several ways. First, it simultaneously explores the "his" and "her" dimensions of international marriage and international migration. It is methodologically unusual because I am studying marriage before spouses actually live together; and I am studying the migration process before the sponsored spouse actually migrates. Second, I start my inquiry with the lives of immigrants in their community of origin, a departure from most research on transnational cultures, which tends to only examine the lives of immigrants after they move. In so doing, I underscore the difficulties undertaken in processes of migration as well as relations with kin left behind in processes of transmigration. Third, this study sheds light on connections among family, gender, and transnationalism in the Vietnamese diaspora, offering a fresh perspective on the out-migration of Vietnamese to Western countries since the mid 1970s. In this sense, I move beyond themes of settlement and acculturation that continue to dominate most research on Vietnamese migration, and provide an important examination of transformations at the family level in the Vietnamese diaspora and in transnational Asia America generally (Freeman 1989, 1995; Kibria 1993; Zhou 1997a, 1997b; Zhou and Bankston 1998).

Chapter 1 introduces the nature of waiting in these marriages, and how married individuals, separated by international space and time, are embedded in historical forces and kin networks.

Chapter 2 focuses specifically on the ability and social struggles of Viet Kieu men who convert low wages from the West to high wages as they return to Vietnam for marriage. The subsequent five chapters (chapters 3 through 7) continue with specific cases of transnational couples in order to illustrate larger themes, structures, and patterns that are involved in Vietnamese international marriages, including issues of gender strategies, matchmaking, money, and the contrasting situations of the "highly marriageables" and the "unmarriageables." The concluding chapter briefly provides some predictions I have for the future of international couples. Readers interested in methodology will find useful the lengthy methodology appendix, which precedes my discussion of the characteristics of the sample in this study. Throughout this book, I purposely move away from the conventional technique of weaving in multiple stories from multiple respondents within each chapter, a practice that often characterizes interview-based or ethnographically informed books and scholarly articles. I have taken this approach so as to provide analytical clarity.

Although I focus on a fairly specific stream of international marriage and migration, this book is not about why Vietnamese people marry other Vietnamese people, nor does it offer a social history of Vietnam. It is also not about why people opt for marriage, as opposed to single status. Ultimately, the implication I make in this book is that international marriages among individuals of the same ethnicity living in different parts of the world are anchored not only in migration histories and colonial pasts but are also motivated by the need for material as well as emotional recuperations of self-worth that make such marriages necessary.

CHAPTER 1

The Gift of Modernity

STORIES ABOUT the cordless telephone cir-
culated for miles. "Every other day during the first month,"
Trang Le, a twenty-seven-year-old college-educated woman,
said calmly, "Someone would come and take a look at it. People,
young and old."[1] Trang told me this on an early evening in
March 2000, when she and I sat in the kitchen of her family's
four-story, six-bedroom house in Dong Huong, a village set
amid the tropical scenery of buffaloes, rice fields, and busy markets in the province of Se Long. I could imagine the parade of
people who wanted to see the modern cordless phone sitting on
the table between us, an ordinary white Panasonic phone that I
confirmed cost a mere $20 at Radio Shack, a well-known elec-
tronic store in the United States. Trang told me that people were
amazed at the cordless technology, which arrived in this village
well before the now ubiquitous cell phone. She explained that
some people were reluctant to hold the expensive gift she had
received from her twenty-nine-year-old husband, Hieu Vu,
who originally sent the gift to her before they were married.[2]
He sent it after they met for the first time in 1996 so that he
could call her regularly—on a daily basis, he initially promised.
His mother, Mrs. Pham, delivered the phone to Trang in 1998
when she traveled to her Vietnam-based home in Dong Huong.
As an immigrant to the United States in 1985, Mrs. Pham had
begun to take these trips back home several years before in order
to care for her mother in Dong Huong. She regularly went back

and forth from Dong Huong to Clear Pine, her U.S.-based home in a quiet suburb outside of Boston.

Hieu was a shy man who used his words sparingly but deliberately. A thin man of roughly 5 foot 7, he always wore neatly ironed trousers and button-down shirts. In February 2001, when I met him in Clear Pine, almost a year after I met Trang in Vietnam, Hieu was working at a local department store where he had just been promoted to assistant supervisor of the inventory room, a position that took him ten years to earn because he only had a high school degree. On our first interview, I asked Hieu about the telephone he sent Trang, even though I had already learned about the social history of the gift from my visits to Trang in Vietnam. Hieu explained that he sent the phone to his wife because he wanted to familiarize her with technologies people enjoy in "modern" countries such as the United States.

Hieu's reason for sending Trang the phone was as strikingly paradoxical as the contrast in their standards of living: Trang, living in a large luxurious house situated in a remote part of the third world, had the best of amenities imported from the West, whereas Hieu resided with his parents near the global city of Boston in a small two-bedroom apartment with barely any furnishings. And whereas Trang's two maids served us elaborate meals during our interviews in the village of Dong Huong, Hieu and I were struggling to keep warm while splitting leftover food he had cooked for the week's workdays in Boston.

Hieu explained that he heard telephone lines in the Dong Huong village had improved dramatically since his first visit to meet Trang in 1996. Most families who live adjacent to the village market (a hint of social and economic status, since markets are the center of village life) have telephones. But Hieu thought Trang would be the first to have a cordless one in the small but crowded riverside hamlet. From his standpoint, the status-laden modern gift, along with other commodities that he regularly sent, let villagers know that he was a good transnational husband.[3] Trang was, indeed, the first in Dong Huong to own a cordless telephone. But the truth, unbeknownst to Hieu, was that she already had one when she was living in Saigon while attending Outerspace, one of many English schools that had sprung up like lotus flowers in the mid-1980s when Vietnam reopened its doors to the world.

Vietnam was not active in the intensifying global economy after the 1970s, because of the social and political turmoil that ended with the fall of Saigon. In 1986, after having no contact with most of the outside world for over a decade, Vietnam adopted a new socioeconomic policy called *Doi Moi* ("changing for the new") which, although it did not end state ownership or central planning, moved the country from complete state-sponsored socialism to partial free-market capitalism (Ebashi 1997; Morley and Nishihara 1997a). The reform was gradual, and the actual pace of the transition to a market economy was slow.

Some observers note that it was not until the mid 1990s that Vietnam actively reentered the global economy under formalized political and economic coalitions with other countries. It was admitted to the Association of Southeast Asian Nations (ASEAN) in 1993 and in August 1995, U.S. President Bill Clinton established full diplomatic relations with the country (Morley and Nishihara 1997b). The normalization of economic and social ties in 1995 eased the movement of culture, goods, and bodies across national borders, and it gradually increased the number of individuals from the Vietnamese diaspora who returned as tourists or to visit family members. The Vietnamese government estimates that currently more than one million overseas Vietnamese return annually for tourism and to visit relatives, a dramatic increase from the 87,000 who came in 1992, and from the only 8,000 who visited in 1988 (Thomas 1997). Furthermore, the United Nations reports that in 2004, overseas Vietnamese remitted about US$3.2 billion, a dramatic increase from only $35 million in 1991 (Nguyen 2002; United Nations 2006). In the same year, 2004, Vietnam also ranked sixteenth among the top remittance-receiving countries worldwide and fifth among all Asian countries after India, China, the Philippines, and Pakistan.

As part of a growing segment of rich rural families in Vietnam, Trang enjoyed numerous aspects of "modernity" that have been fueled by this very culture of remittance, and which have been made possible, in part, by a series of international out-migrations by members of Trang's kin network as well as by the recent government policy shift. Trang's father, Mr. Le, was living in the United States when I met Trang. He migrated in 1991, leaving his wife and five children behind in Dong Huong, as part of the Humanitarian Operation Program of 1989, an official agreement between the United States and the Socialist Republic of Vietnam that allowed Vietnamese political prisoners, current and former detainees (and their families) in reeducation camps, to migrate to the United States. Over 70,000 people have arrived under the Humanitarian Operation Program of 1989, constituting the largest category of Vietnamese refugees admitted to the United States since 1990. Unlike Vietnamese "boat" refugees of the late 1970s and 1980s, who often came with only the clothes on their backs, the "HO," as they are referred to in Vietnamese American communities, migrated and continue to migrate to the United States on comfortable modern jetliners to established communities where they have relatives who can provide social and financial support (Zhou and Bankston 1998).

Mr. Le's younger brother Tan was one of those late 1970s boat people, who later migrated to Toronto. And, as Trang's father's only sibling, Tan had generously contributed financially to the family for over a decade. Thus, Trang and her family luxuriated in an unusually large house that was built several miles down the road from a raisin factory, the source of their new wealth, that they started with the help of Tan's remittances. The diasporic objects in their house were lucid symbols of a family actively involved in global and transmigratory processes. They had, for example, a bathroom sink made in Germany, an electronic rice pot from Taiwan, bedroom décor imported from Japan, picture frames given to them by relatives in Australia, and now the white Panasonic cordless telephone from the United States.

In 1991, Trang's parents sent Trang and her younger brother to Saigon for a university education, a common practice among aspiring and well-to-do families in villages all over the Mekong Delta's twelve provinces. During those college years, Trang and her brother stayed with their mother's eldest sister, whose husband also had many relatives living abroad. Trang simultaneously enrolled in the prestigious Ho Chi Minh City College of Economics and the Outerspace English School, with hopes of one day working for one of the foreign companies in Vietnam that burgeoned in the early 1990s—not for the financial rewards (her family gave her that), but for the social circles she thought she would be able to join. After her college training, Trang was one of the many well-trained students in Saigon—although one of the very few women—who acquired international business and language skills, but found that no company would hire them. In the mid 1990s, foreign companies that had arrived in earlier years packed up and left Vietnam, in part because of the Asian economic crisis that occurred during this time, but also in part because many companies were dissatisfied with profit margins in Vietnam as well as the heavy taxes and bureaucratic trials they had to confront in order to start up businesses (Fforde and Vylder 1996; Han and Baumgarte 2000; Keenan 1997; Murray 1997; Sidel 1999; Thayer and Amer 2000). With no other opportunities in sight, Trang returned to her village of Dong Huong in 1996 to assist her parents with the raisin factory, a company that produced for markets all over the Asia-Pacific region. The English and business skills that Trang picked up in Saigon were useful, as she and her parents discovered. Trang began to negotiate business matters with people—usually men—from Singapore and China, where English was the language of business. Trang told me that some of these men bought raisins from her family's factory and then resold them on the world market. Well before I met them, Trang and her family were global business people and transnational villagers of a particular kind.

THE PERSONAL DIMENSIONS
OF GLOBALIZATION

Students of globalization can extract multiple themes from tracing the development of transnational villagers and global factories like the one owned by Trang's family in Dong Huong. Researchers of economic development, for instance, might show how such rural agricultural economies utilize remittances to participate in the global economy. Theorists of applied economics might be able to explain how world markets constrain or produce profits for a raisin factory in the Vietnamese province of Se Long, in comparison with a similar factory in, say, rural China. Trang certainly relied on such economic theories when she negotiated with other business people, for example, about how much to charge for a certain quantity of raisins or which packaging method was most profitable during a particular season. She developed a complex system of accounting that measured profit margins and productivity on the basis of the applied economics she learned in the Ho Chi Minh City College of Economics, which is similar to what students might learn anywhere about international business transactions.

But after the work day ended, globalization and phrases like "international markets" took on different meanings for Trang. During the day, when Trang negotiated in the world of business, globalization was for the most part impersonal. It was her work.

In her spare time, when the work was over, when English was no longer the language of communication, globalization became local and personal. It became her life as she reflected on her international marriage to Hieu, an overseas Vietnamese man who had not benefited from migration as much as his parents had hoped, but who took part in global processes in ways that are much more difficult to measure than the raisin factory that Trang's parents owned. The international marriage between Trang and Hieu thus showcases a significant, but often hidden, tale of globalization, going far beyond cordless phones, raisins, or any other diasporic commodity.

Marriage in a Changing Time

In many ways, Trang's marriage began prior to but was also made possible by her father's emigration to the United States in 1991. Trang's father knew that his twenty-seven-year-old daughter, the eldest of five children, was a cautiously choosy person in all matters. According to Trang's mother, Mrs. Liem, her father often joked that Trang, despite being a village "girl," had tastes and styles that surpassed those of any young woman in Saigon.[4] And probably, from their comparative standpoints, Trang was also picky among young women in Paris, Los Angeles, Toronto, or Sydney—four "global" cities where their family had at least one relative who left Vietnam after the post-war years. In my conversations with Trang's parents, they admitted that they were "semi-modern" people, compared to their fellow villagers who often wanted to arrange marriages for their children. This ambivalent modernity was reflected, for instance, in Trang's mother's choice of clothing. While they had some of the most advanced technology in their house, Trang's mother wore traditional dress, not being comfortable in the "modern" clothing such as the blue jeans that Trang preferred, and she insisted we meet in the formal living area rather than in the kitchen where the family mostly gathered, and where Trang and I first met.

When asked, Trang's parents qualified their gender ideology (Hochschild 1989, 15) as "semi-modern" because, for their eldest son's wife, they chose someone from their village, anticipating that they, the older couple, would live indefinitely with their children.[5] For reasons rooted in complicated and traditional geographical practices of kinship, they wanted their eldest daughter-in-law to be near her parents. They also felt that a village "girl," but not a village "boy," could certainly be an in-law, for they felt that a daughter-in-law is someone who mostly does domestic work, a skill they did not have to look too far to find. In this family, as has been the case in many Vietnamese families with emergent transnational and remittance ties, the social standards for daughters-in-law have largely remained unchanged, whereas the expectations for sons-in-law have risen in recent years.

Among the newly affluent of Vietnam—many of whom, though certainly not all, are part of transnational families— expectations about education, income, and family assets have risen for grooms, though not for brides. This is, in part, because the number of women acquiring higher education and earning an income, from remittances or otherwise, has risen in the past decade (Nguyen and Thomas 2004; Turner and Nguyen 2005), which means that these women and their families continue to "marry up as they move up," whereas most men continue to insist on "marrying down" even as they move up economically and socially. In other words, the prevailing and nearly universal "marriage gradient" norm of women marrying down and men marrying up continues, as usual, for some families in this local and cultural context, despite the fact that the income and education gap between young men and women is gradually narrowing. Although their own marriage and that of their eldest son were arranged, Trang's parents once hoped that Trang would "choose" her husband while away at college in Saigon, for they felt early on that no village boy could meet Trang's expectations for a husband. Even more important, they saw no one in Dong Huong or the province of Se Long who met their expectations for a son-in-law. This was perhaps the "traditional" side of Trang's parents' semi-modern gender ideology, for while they accepted that their son married down, they expected that their daughter would marry up.

Though it had not always been the case, Trang's parents emerged as highly respected villagers in Dong Huong. Since marriage in Vietnam is an important matter not only because it unites two people but also because it establishes significant ties of obligations for extended networks of kin (Tran 1991), Trang's parents were aware of the many eyes that watched as their eldest daughter took careful steps into the market of marriage and intimacy. Families moving up any Vietnamese ladder of respect or honor often move their children, especially daughters, out of certain segments of a silent, yet, highly castelike marriage market. This is because men in Vietnam, influenced, if only partly, by traditional notions of hierarchies based on gender, age, and class, more often than not wish to "marry down" socially and economically.

Trang's parents were certainly near, if not at the top of, the respect ladder. And they wanted to maintain that respect. Thus, under the persuasive advice of his Toronto-based brother, Tan, Trang's father saw no reason for the entire family to uproot themselves and leave Vietnam for a potentially downwardly mobile life in the United States when they were presented with the opportunity to migrate as a whole family unit in 1991. Therefore, as part of a binational split-household strategy, Trang's mother stayed in Vietnam with all her children to continue with their successful raisin factory, while Trang's father migrated by himself through the H.O. program. Once he became a Viet Kieu, Trang's father explored various social facets of Vietnamese

America, which gradually led to the international marriage arrangement for Trang and Hieu.

In recent years, participants in Viet Kieu remittance circles have geographically expanded their marriage options. Upwardly mobile men move from one locale to another in search of more suitable brides, even as they continue to embrace the prevailing norm of the marriage gradient. But in Vietnam, whereas men seeking wives in the milieu of globalization are limited for the most part to the marriage market in Vietnam, women have increasingly gone global in the search for husbands. This, in part, has to do with the fact that virtually all Viet Kieu and other "foreigners" returning and going to Vietnam seeking marriage partners are men, rather than women. Thus, the intensification of economic globalization in Vietnam in the late 1980s and 1990s rapidly opened up impersonal markets of capital, goods, and labor, and in conjunction with these markets, it also opened up a gendered personal market of emotions and marriages. Like global corporations and factories that recently moved to Vietnam because of its large supply of labor, male Viet Kieu are returning to Vietnam in search of brides because it provides a much larger selection of potential marriage partners.

A Quiet Double-Gender Movement

Trang and Hieu participated in what I call the Vietnamese double-gender movement, a movement among men in the diaspora and women in Vietnam to postpone or resist marriages with their local counterparts and subsequently to globalize their marriage options. They represented a distinct pattern in the Asian diaspora, one rooted in specific political and social histories among nation-states. Trang felt early on not only that village men were too traditional [*truyen thong*] along principles of gender but also that Saigonese men were slow to join women like her in the quest for gender equity in marital and family life. She saw her brother marry a fellow villager, someone who finished high school, an adequate marker of excellence and respectability in the female version of educational expectations in village life. In Dong Huong, as is the case for most places worldwide, there is a "his" and a "her" version of marriage choices (Bernard 1972).

These asymmetrical versions of marriage choices made it acceptable for Trang's brother to marry someone "below" him, but not so for her to do the same. As a woman, Trang publicly expressed desires to marry up, the result of pressure from family and friends. Yet, privately, as Trang explained to me, she was not overly picky about a man's economic and educational status. Like many single people, Trang had a list of qualities she wanted in a marital partner, the most important of which was that, at a minimum, she wanted to marry a man who would, as she told me, respect her and respect "modernization and equality for women [*hien dai va su binh dang cho phu nu*]." Few women married to local men I met in Vietnam thought about this aspect of marital life because, for better or for worse, marriage is still one of the key routes that women in Vietnam take in order to acquire economic security outside of their natal family. But Trang priced herself out of certain marriage markets when she chose a higher education in Saigon, particularly because she came from a well-to-do family in one of Vietnam's villages. She was caught in a marriage gradient paradox: few men in Vietnam "below" her wanted to marry a highly educated woman, yet, there were few available single men in the village who were socially or economically "above" her, since the latter group of men were married well before Trang edged into the marriage market.

In some ways, Trang went with her public marriage preference. She searched for an upward marriage, but she did this in a market where there were few available single men who were more educated or whose family fared economically better than hers. She remained single during her stint as a college student in Saigon, dating only casually, as most Saigonese young adults are now doing. For Trang, even the "modernized" Saigonese men were still held back by gender traditions, such as men's resistance to having employed wives and to sharing housework equally, that she wanted to abolish. To be sure, Trang said that in her observation, there were some men, the *hiem* or "rare" ones, who treated their girlfriends equitably. At best, though, when she talked at length about these rare men, they sounded like "transitional men," men who were largely confused in changing times about their beliefs in "traditional" and "egalitarian" marriages, and who often straddled uncomfortably between the two (Hochschild 1989). Few men, according to Trang, had responded to a Vietnamese version of a "female revolt" against unsatisfying and unequal relationships (Hite 1988). She told me that her best, yet elusive, marriage option in Vietnam was to marry one of the "rare" men, a transitional at best. Among other reasons, but mostly because she was embedded in a transnational network, Trang saw the choice to expand her marriage options globally.

Transnational Family Ties in the Global Marriage Market

Shortly after Trang's father arrived in the United States in 1991, he visited and then resided with Tan, his brother in Toronto. Soon Trang's father had confirmed stories that he had heard while still in the Mekong Delta about the circumstances of men in the Vietnamese diaspora. In contemporary Vietnam, Viet Kieu men are invariably viewed as belonging to two distinct groups: the "successful [*thanh cong*]," who moved up the Viet Kieu economic ladder by owning ethnic enterprises or by obtaining an education, and the "indolent [*luoi bieng*]" without full-time jobs, who are perceived as welfare dependents or participants in underground economies, such as gambling. Some see the latter group as men who took up valuable migration "spots" that others could have filled. Many men in Vietnam told me different fantasies with the same plot. "If I had gotten a chance to go," it usually began, "I would be so rich by now."

Mr. Le, Trang's father, felt proud that his brother had risked migration and achieved this upper tier; this meant that Mr. Le did not face postmigration difficulties that pervade the experiences of contemporary migrants to the United States, especially those from Southeast Asia. Such difficulties include minimal social support in postmigrant communities, mental and emotional difficulties from living in refugee camps, and social displacements in places with no ethnic communities (Booth, Crouter, and Landale 1997; Kibria 1993; Ong and Liu 1994; Portes and McLeod 1996; Zhou and Bankston 1998). Mr. Le did not participate in a labor or a family reunification program, two of the dominant mechanisms for contemporary migration to the United States. Rather, as an H.O. migrant, he was a subject and a manifestation of a historical political relationship between nation-states. He was part of an exile culture, yet he was also fortunate enough to have been part of a remittance culture prior to his migration.

Trang told me that her father arrived in Toronto wearing a necktie and Dockers pants (made and bought in Vietnam), already prepared to assist his Toronto-based brother in managing real estate properties. He initially depended on the reverse remittances that his wife sent him from the Mekong Delta with the income from their raisin factory. At the time that I met the family in the Mekong Delta, he had not yet started sending financial remittances to Vietnam. But he had an important social remittance to offer (Levitt 2001b). In his first year living overseas, Mr. Le called his wife to tell her about a "nice boy" he met in Clear Pine, Massachusetts.

Mr. Le knew that it was not his usual family role to step into his daughter's marital decisions. In traditional Vietnamese households, there are representatives for "her" and for "him," with fathers more likely to intervene in their son's marriage decisions and, conversely, mothers serving as consultants for daughters. Mr. Le became involved in his daughter's international marriage arrangement because his brother, Tan, had known Hieu from Clear Pine for many years. Tan was one of the many single men who independently left Vietnam in the late 1970s and throughout the 1980s, and who later found themselves in refugee camps such as the Ban Napho camp in Thailand, where Tan was "processed." There in Ban Napho, he met Hieu's family and was adopted as a fictive kin, a common survival strategy among the residents of refugee camps. Hieu's father and Tan were "refugee buddies [*ban ti nan*]." Although a combination of serendipity and social capital moved these two men along different routes of class mobility, Tan knew that Hieu came from a good family living in the United States—honest, hard-working, and humble. Tan had known Hieu since the boy was only seven in the refugee camp and had watched him grow up over the years, albeit from a distance. Hieu had shared with Tan his difficulty in finding a Vietnamese wife in Clear Pine and the loneliness of being in Middle America as a young immigrant man. Tan wanted to help Hieu find a wife, because he understood the pain of prolonged single status—something he endured until not too long before, when he also returned to Vietnam at the age of forty-one for a wife.

Deep in Tan's gender ideology were other reasons for encouraging his brother (Trang's father) to arrange a marriage for Hieu and Trang. Tan was genuinely concerned that his niece would face permanent single status in Vietnam, since he felt she was getting old by Vietnamese standards. But beneath those concerns, Tan had his own agenda in mind. He felt that Viet Kieu women offered little respect to Viet Kieu men in married life. So while Trang quietly joined women in Vietnam in a female movement resisting marriage to nonegalitarian Vietnamese men,

Hieu was part of a male movement resisting marriage to a perceived population of "overly modern" women in overseas Vietnamese communities. Hieu and Trang were leading parallel lives, as they were part of two gender movements that pushed them into overlapping orbits. Trang was part of a movement among some single women in Vietnam and Hieu was part of a movement among some single men in the Vietnamese diaspora, two movements to postpone or resist marriages with their local counterparts and to search globally for marriage partners. They both searched not only for marriage but also for a gendered version of respect and social worth that each thought the other side would be ready and willing to give.

This double-gender movement is anchored in at least three socioeconomic patterns throughout the Vietnamese diaspora. First, as with most postmigrant communities, Vietnamese men in the diaspora have found that they can no longer expect or practice traditional gender arrangements in family and intimate relationships, particularly, as I will detail, among those working in low-wage jobs who cannot afford their part of the bargain with patriarchy (Kandiyoti 1988). Second, overseas women have gained socioeconomic power relative to men and relative to their premigration experiences, both of which no longer situate men as the only economic provider in Vietnamese families (Kibria 1993). And finally, social and economic remittances from overseas together with enhanced employment and educational opportunities in contemporary Vietnam have prompted some women to postpone or avoid marriages with local men. While Trang and her friends postponed or refused marriages with local men in Vietnam, overseas Vietnamese men like Hieu refused marriages with local Viet Kieu women. With Tan's initiation, encouragement, and financial assistance, Hieu went to Vietnam and met Trang soon after his future father-in-law arrived in the United States. Trang and Hieu were introduced in 1996, and the two married within two years.

When I met Trang in 2000, she was waiting in Vietnam for legal clearance to migrate to the United States and to join Hieu in Clear Pine. The couple had been married for well over seventeen months, and yet they had not been able to clear migration paperwork for her to join him there. Hieu held only a green card as a permanent resident; he had yet to become a citizen of the United States, a status that the couple did not fully realize would put them at a severe disadvantage for sponsoring Trang's migration. They not only had to wait longer than other international couples where the "sponsoring" spouse is a U.S. citizen, but a U.S. Immigration and Naturalization Service quota system limiting how many spouses could be sponsored by green card holders meant that they had to wait indefinitely (United States Department of Homeland Security 2006; USINS 2002).[6] Although U.S. immigration policy sets no limitations on how many "foreign" spouses of American citizens can migrate to the United States, foreign spouses of green card holders are second in a complicated "preference system" for family reunification (United States Department of Homeland Security 2006).

During this waiting period, Trang and Hieu proceeded with their lives, modeling their transnational split-household arrangement after the one organized by Trang's parents. At the time that I met him, Hieu had returned to Vietnam twice with his father-in-law since he and Trang married in early 1998, staying for over six weeks each time. The cordless telephone that Hieu bought from his department store as a gift for Trang was a symbol of the paradoxical reality of contemporary Vietnamese international marriages. Hieu and Trang had different reasons for participating in the marriage, but the long distance separating the newlyweds meant that they did not disclose those reasons to each other, as I discovered when I interviewed each in their separate countries. What I discovered during my visit with Trang was that she wanted more than just a modern telephone. She wanted a modern man.[7]

CHAPTER 2

Convertibility

TEO DOAN was a thirty-two-year-old man who worked for his parents at a small sandwich shop in the heart of San Jose's Silicon Valley, where the second highest concentration of Viet Kieu outside of Vietnam reside. Thirty-year-old Toan Pham was the afternoon janitor at a public elementary school in urban Los Angeles, the metropolitan area with the highest concentration of Viet Kieu in the diaspora. Both men wanted to marry women of Vietnamese origin, but despite their demographic advantage of living in heavily populated Vietnamese metropolitan areas, both returned to Vietnam for wives with the arrangements of family and kin throughout the Vietnamese diaspora. The stories of Teo and Toan illuminate why and how some immigrant men of color, particularly those in low-wage work, pursue convertibility of low income across national boundaries to claim a sense of self-worth as they seek marriages in their community of origin. This international convertibility allows these men, in turn, to feel, if not become, more marriageable in the global hierarchy of marriage markets.

Upon their return to Vietnam for marriage, low-wage immigrant men like Toan and Teo engage in small-scale conspicuous consumption, such as everyday drinking and eating activities and employing simple gift-giving practices that are often beyond their means in the West. This convertibility becomes most meaningful when they establish and maintain translocal relations that "are constituted within historically and geographically specific points of origin and migration established by transmigrants," and thereby form a "triadic connection that links transmigrants, the localities to which they migrate, and their locality of origin" (Guarnizo and Smith 1998, 13). Convertibility across national borders benefits Vietnamese immigrant men by offering them the ability to cross international borders to go from the status of low marriageability to high marriageability. To be sure, both men and women of the diaspora pursue convertibility of economic capital when they return to Vietnam. Likewise, men from across social class backgrounds also take part in convertibility, which is to say that convertibility across social fields was important for both working-class as well as middle-class men. But the interrelated issues of global convertibility, social status, and masculinity are particularly central, salient, and relevant to the lives of low-wage immigrant men. This is especially true when one considers that about 80 percent of the men in my sample of sixty-nine marriages were low-wage working men who, because of their low-wage status, have found it difficult to find marriage partners in their overseas locations. These men viewed their jobs as not respectable, which they felt also made them unmarriageable in the overseas location, a fact that prompted them to seek an international marriage from the country of origin.

In many ways, men like Teo and Toan were at the bottom in terms of social status among men in their local overseas contexts, in part because Vietnamese American men earn on average 30 percent less than their white counterparts, and they are one of the lowest income-earning ethnic groups in the United States (Yamane 2001). Most of the men entered low-paying jobs after migration that, as Teo said, only allowed them "to survive [*de song*]." Except for a few men who worked in ethnic enterprises such as nail salons, where average hourly wages ranged from $8 to $12 per hour, I refer to Vietnamese American low-wage men in this study as men who generally earned on average between

$6 to $8 per hour. These men usually worked in hourly wage, secondary labor-market jobs that offered them little stability (Sakamoto and Chen 1991). Their yearly salaries ranged between $8,000 and $24,000, and many of them fell below the U.S. poverty level at the time I conducted fieldwork (Dalaker 2001). Yet, these wages are at the top globally when compared to their male counterparts in contemporary Vietnam, since wages in the United States are exponentially higher than those in Vietnam. For example, at the time of my research for this project, 2 million Vietnamese dongs (VND 2 million = US$133) was considered the typical wage per month in Vietnam among professionals such as foreign translators, pharmacists, and even some medical doctors. Thus, while some of the low-wage men in this study experienced tremendous downward social and economic mobility after migration, their low wage overseas takes on different economic and social meanings when they return to Vietnam.

TRANSNATIONAL CULTURAL CORNERS

I met Teo about an hour's drive south of San Francisco in the Vietnamese enclave of the Silicon Valley, where Teo grew up as the middle child in a relatively comfortable home. Teo lived with his parents in a 1950s-built tract home nestled behind the Lion Plaza, the popular Vietnamese shopping center at the corner of Tully and King roads. Both of his parents drove brand new Honda Accords, and Teo frequently borrowed them, as he did not have a car himself. His parents' lifestyle, as exhibited by the house they lived in and the cars they drove, indicated that they were at least economically middle class. Their consumption patterns demonstrated, in part, how they claimed a sense of worth. As Lisa Park (2005) argues, social citizenship, anchored in questions of national belonging among some immigrants, particularly those who work in labor-intensive entrepreneurial enterprise, is often asserted through conspicuous consumption. But because Teo's parents, both in their late fifties, owned a simple sandwich shop that catered to the mixed-income ethnic community in which they lived, Teo thought of his parents' work, and by extension of himself—since he also worked at the shop—as part of the working class [*tang lop lao dong*]. Each day, his parents woke up at four A.M. to prepare for the shop's early opening hour, and they worked there at least until after eight P.M. The "style" [*kieu*] of their lives, as Teo emphasized, is one of "laborers who work with our hands so we can have enough to survive."

Teo had internalized his style of living in his early adulthood. A "magnified moment" was realized when his older brother and younger sister both earned educational credentials to secure office jobs. Arlie Russell Hochschild defines "magnified moments" as "episodes of heightened importance, either epiphanies, moments of intense glee or unusual insight, or moments in which things go intensely but meaningfully wrong. In either case, the moment stands out; it is metaphorically rich, unusually elaborate and often echoes" (1994, 4). Indeed, magnified moments in the everyday lives of respondents in this study offer an important window into the worlds of decisions and understanding about international marriages. Because Teo did not have an office job, as he explained, he had unofficially assumed responsibility for his parents' elderly years, in place of his brother who was two years older. He assumed this responsibility, in part, because he was also working for his parents at the sandwich shop and still living in their home (which saved him a tremendous amount of money in the expensive Silicon Valley). This was partly an economic exchange for Teo, since he did not have viable alternatives, and working at his parents' sandwich shop seemed to be a better option than obtaining a low-wage job that offered little autonomy. As Teo told me, "I work whenever I want and can take vacations whenever I want."

When Teo spoke about his brother, he spoke with a sense of discomfort about the fact that his brother and his brother's wife were both professionals. "They are very critical people [*phe binh*]," he revealed. Teo said that they criticized him for not earning a college degree, and as a result, called him unmarriageable. Yet, when I was able to persuade him to talk about his romantic history, Teo was moderately confident about his ability to court women in the United States and, like many men in this study, he made sure to let me know that he did not go to Vietnam to marry because he was simply *e* or "unmarketable," a term that frequently refers to commodities at markets that remain unsold, and is also often used metaphorically to stigmatize those of marriageable age and not yet married. Teo went a little further than most men, however, by taking out photo albums to show me pictures of him with about half a dozen ex-girlfriends, all of whom were Vietnamese Americans, taken throughout his early adulthood, as if to offer evidence of his masculinity and marriageability. When we spoke at length about the last serious relationship, Teo explained that it was a difficult breakup "for her." As I continued in this line of inquiry, I learned that it took Teo two years to realize that he was "over [*xong*]" the relationship. He met this ex-girlfriend at the community college, in the Vietnamese Student Association, in 1988 when he was nineteen. She courted him more aggressively, according to him, than he courted her. They had a romantic beginning, and he even bragged that they once took a trip together to Hawaii—something he felt only married people do.

Two years after they started dating, Teo was at best halfway through his community college education, while the ex-girlfriend excelled and was accepted into one of the best University of California campuses. They remained committed to each other while she went to the university, but he felt she lost interest at a point when she was accepted into another UC school to earn her pharmacy degree. He said he always felt comfortable going out with her UC friends, but she did not like to meet or go out with his community college friends—a sign of disrespect to him. According to Teo, he eventually broke up the relationship, because he felt that she lost interest in him. "She was fine with the breakup," Teo explained, "But I know she was in pain." Several more visits with Teo revealed that he had broken up that serious relationship because he could not envision himself marrying a woman who he felt had so much more education than he did. As he explained to me: "I know I should be happy if my wife is successful, but when the wife feels she is better than the husband, it is not a good situation [*mot hoan canh khong tot*]. My ex-girlfriend and I almost got married, but I think she did not feel easy with me not having an advanced college education. And you know how Vietnamese people are; they are very snobby if they have advanced degrees like they only care about *si* [doctorates]."

Teo's ability to court women in his early adulthood did not follow him through his early thirties, when people he knew began to earn "careers" rather than the sort of job that Teo took in the enclave and secondary labor markets. When he felt his last ex-girlfriend did not "respect" him because of his lack of higher education, Teo began to look elsewhere for a marriage partner. "As a man," Teo said to me with a strong sense of conviction, "you have to have a certain kind of status." But as Teo looked elsewhere in the highly populated Vietnamese enclave of the Silicon Valley, he found that social status was relatively difficult to achieve regardless of what social circles he entered, for he was still a sandwich maker wherever he maneuvered himself. "Vietnamese people here [in the U.S.] only pay attention to how much money you make or what kind of degrees you have," Teo said. "The women don't want to marry men who don't have comfortable jobs."

When Teo began to look seriously for marriage prospects, he moved out of his Silicon Valley cultural corner and, in effect, turned to a transnational space in which he could convert his relatively low social status. Like virtually all international couples who relied on transnational networks for marriage arrangements, Teo had one best friend, Manh, who had a single younger sister still living in Vietnam. According to Teo, Manh, also a low-wage worker, had been to Vietnam several times and had each time persuaded Teo to take the trip with him, in part because Manh had wanted to arrange a marriage for Teo with his younger sister. The two men took the first trip together in 1998, and by early 1999, Teo had married Manh's younger sister. When I asked Teo to chronicle that first trip back to Vietnam, he immediately raised the issue of convertibility: "I felt like a different person when I went to Vietnam for the first time, like I had another life in another world. Everything was so cheap, and I could just spend money on luxuries. I didn't have to worry about the cost of anything, like you can take twenty people out to eat a huge feast and it could cost you less than what you would spend on two people in San Jose. It's very luxurious [*sung suong lam*]!"

Teo's relatively low income of barely more than $1,500 per month did not go far in the United States, especially in the expensive Silicon Valley, and this low income was partly a reflection of his level of education. Both the low income and the absence of a college degree in the United States meant that Teo felt he had little opportunity for social mobility in the formal U.S. labor market, and in Teo's eyes, to acquire social status, particularly in the Vietnamese American marriage market. Like many Viet Kieu who journey home, Teo converted his low income to take pleasure in luxuries that he could not usually afford in the United States, like taking "twenty people out to eat a huge feast." The immediate convertibility of money is linked immediately to the convertibility of status and esteem.

This process of convertibility allows men like Teo to participate in a marriage market where they feel they have something to offer, and which they, in turn, feel could offer them something. As Teo explained:

> In America, I don't have any *hang* [class/rank], because I only work as a laborer [*nguoi lao dong*], but when I go to Vietnam, I only need to spend a few hundred dollars and people see the value in me [*gia tri*]. In America, single women see me as nothing because I have nothing. In Vietnam, I have a lot. I can drink and eat much more with the money I make in America than if I try to spend it there. . . . I think it is better [*tot hon*] that I married someone in Vietnam, because we can try to spend more of our time there. We both have family there, and they don't judge me because of my education. In Vietnam, it's all about money, you know [*cai gi cung la tien*].

When men like Teo talked about consumption and being in Vietnam, it was most often in the context of being under the watchful eyes of family and kin. Like Mexicans in the United States whom Luin Goldring described in her study of transmigrants, low-wage Vietnamese immigrant men orient their lives to their place of origin because the "locality of origin provides a unique social and spatial context within transnational communities for making claims to and valorizing social status" (1998, 165). The place of origin thus provides an important social space to which immigrants can return to in order to improve their social position on the basis of material consumption, which is often translated to social power, since purchasing abilities differ enormously between unequal nation-states in the global economy. The anchoring of transnational ties to specific communities of origin meant that Teo operated under a specific social field to validate his social worth. As Teo explained what seems to be a need for an audience of convertibility:

> When you are a Viet Kieu, people in Vietnam watch you. They want to see that you have the ability [*kha nang*] to buy what they cannot. And if you cannot, they will think of you as one of them. And then you are a useless [*vo dung*] Viet Kieu. If you love your family, you also want to show them that you can afford what they cannot, that you can take care of them. . . . But for yourself, you also don't want to have a reputation [*tieng tam*] of someone who cannot buy the things they cannot. Like me, I have been gone for over fifteen years so I have to show that I did something important. I don't want to be a useless Viet Kieu.

THE LOWEST WAGE AMONG LOW-WAGE WORKERS

Among the low-wage men, there were different types of economic "lowness." If income level and the type of work each man did were associated with their sense of self-worth, then the lowest of the low had internalized their low status in compelling ways; lowest-wage men tended to dissociate themselves socially and economically from their overseas community as one approach to avoid being contextualized and compared with other overseas Vietnamese. As Ketu Katrak succinctly describes some transmigrants, they "live here in body and elsewhere in mind and imagination" (1996, 125). This was especially true among the most recent arrivals, like thirty-year-old Toan Pham who, because of the timing of his migration, had more concrete and tangible connections with people in Vietnam than those men who had been gone for longer periods.

I met Toan one weekday afternoon in January 2001 at an inner-city elementary school in urban Los Angeles where he worked as the after-school janitor. Lowest-wage men like Toan frequently perceived their jobs, which usually paid barely the legal minimum wage and sometimes less, as sites of degradation. "It is maybe better not to work at all," as Toan told me, "then to work at a job where you feel humiliated [*nhuc*] to tell people you know." Prior to migrating to the United States in 1996, Toan had a serious relationship with a woman he met when he was in eighth grade, from his home village in the province of Se Long. When Toan left Vietnam through the sponsorship of his father, who was also living in California, he said he did not have the intention of keeping the long-distance relationship with this girlfriend from Se Long. But after being in the United States for only a few months, Toan soon realized that his prospect for marriage in the United States was low, in large part because of his low-wage job. As Toan explained:

> I know I came to America late and that is why I have to work like a buffalo in this school, clean the toilet. There is no status with society in this job. No woman will want to marry a man like me. I can barely make enough money to feed myself, how can I provide for a woman in America? No woman here will respect me for what I do. If I married a woman here, she will get tired of seeing me with this job and she will leave me. If a woman does not respect what you do, she won't respect you. And what kind of marriage will you have if there is no respect?

Thus after having been in the United States for only two years, Toan returned to Vietnam to propose marriage, having kept in touch with his serious girlfriend in Se Long. Like my interviews with most men in this study, I asked Toan to recount his feelings and experiences with the first visit home. "We live overseas, we have nothing. We just work. When we go to Vietnam, we have happiness [*co su sung suong*]. [Why?] Because we have money when we go to Vietnam. There are people who will look at us, people who will pay attention to us because we have a behavior of a person [*tu cach con nguoi*] that is enough for others to have a relation with [*quan he*], we are not an ordinary person [*nguoi tam tuong*] [in Vietnam]."

Indeed, as a janitor in Los Angeles, Toan viewed himself as an "ordinary person," someone who was embarrassed to tell people what he did for a wage, for in the landscape of urban Los Angeles, Toan's income of $6.75 an hour meant that he could not afford the sort of lifestyle in Los Angeles that he enjoyed whenever he visited Vietnam. I have heard and witnessed hundreds of stories of Viet Kieu who made barely minimum wages in their overseas homes, but who consumed extravagantly when they visited Vietnam. As Toan succinctly confessed his consumption habits, "In America, I often spend a whole day thinking about whether I should go and eat a five dollar bowl of *pho* [beef noodle soup] when I get off work, but in Vietnam, I don't even think twice when I go to a bar or café and pay 2 million Vietnamese dongs [US$133] for a bottle of Hennessy [cognac]."

One of the most striking observations on the question of convertibility across national boundaries has been made by Espiritu, who compellingly argues that it is not often possible to use standard measures such as education or occupation to talk about class status among transnational and immigrant populations. As she suggests in her study of the Filipino community in San Diego, the class status of most of her informants was both ambiguous and transnational: "I met Filipinos/as who toiled as assembly workers but who, through the pooling of income and finances, owned homes in middle-class communities. . . . I encountered individuals who struggled economically in the United States but owned sizable properties in the Philippines. And I interviewed immigrants who continued to view themselves as 'upper class' even while living in dire conditions in the United States" (2003, 20)

How is the convertibility of money, status, and consumption across transnational social fields related to marriage choices?

If Teo felt that an absence of a college degree meant that he could not earn respect by marrying the ex-girlfriend who was heading for a pharmacy degree, then Toan's very low-wage job led him to believe that he was completely unmarriageable in the United States, which made it necessary for him to return to Vietnam for marriage. "If I want to find a wife in the U.S.," Toan said, "I will have to wait for the next life [*kiep sau*]." Both Teo and Toan felt marginal in their overseas marriage markets, although in different ways. Whereas Teo sensed that he deliberately rejected the marriage market in the United States, Toan felt he was rejected. But their two experiences of rejections were anchored in the same way as the two men sought to participate in small-scale conspicuous consumption in Vietnam: they returned to Vietnam in order to convert their low U.S. incomes to high Vietnam income, and in the process of convertibility, they made themselves more marriageable in the Vietnamese global hierarchy of marriage markets. Some men like Teo and Toan were successful at achieving their goals, of upgrading their sense of self-worth, but convertibility across transnational social fields came at a cost that often resulted in sacrifices at the everyday level in their overseas contexts.

As Le Anh Tu Packard observes, "over time, stereotypical images of rich, ostentatious and arrogant Viet Kieu on the one side, and of ignorant, backward, and beggarly 'country bumpkins' on the other, have been replaced by more nuanced views" (1999, 82). Indeed, the initial views about overseas Vietnamese by Vietnamese nationals were that Viet Kieu had an impressive purchasing power because of income differences between Vietnam and the West. Although initial views have not been changed entirely, they have gradually been transformed as locals learn that while the high Viet Kieu salaries could purchase a luxury life in Vietnam, they could not go far in the West. Thus men like Teo and Toan gradually realized that in order to keep up with their images of Viet Kieu who are "ready to play" [*trieu choi*], they must spend every last bit of savings on the few weeks or months that they visit Vietnam, while they live with minimal lives in their overseas locations for the rest of the year. They, in effect, reverse their worlds of consumption.

Thus, the most basic contradiction of convertibility across transnational social fields is that materially men like Toan live a first-world life in Vietnam, and a third-world life in the United States. As Toan, like many Viet Kieu, succinctly explained this reversion to me, "I abstain from eating and drinking [*nhin an nhin uong*] as much as possible in the United States so that I can live like a king when I go to Vietnam." This meant, for example, that Toan survived on the most basic needs when he resides in Los Angeles, in part, he said, "because there is no one to look at you and judge what you eat and drink." Toan told me that in Los Angeles, he ate instant ramen noodles for dinner at least three or four times a week, packed all his lunches for work, and rarely ate at a restaurant. In contrast, he said, in Vietnam "instant noodles are for the poor," and as a Viet Kieu he needed to demonstrate his ability to pay for expensive food items, like jumbo shrimp or abalone shellfish—two items he said he never consumed in the United States. As Toan explained the social meanings of consumption in the West and in Vietnam, "When I am in Vietnam, people know that I have money, and they expect me to pay for everything. It is embarrassing when a Viet Kieu goes back to Vietnam, and he is cheap [*keo*]. And you can never let anyone in Vietnam pay for you when you go back there. People expect you to be able to afford anything [*nghi rang co du kha nang*]."

Thus, in order to recuperate from their loss of status in their overseas locations, low-wage Vietnamese immigrant men attempt to live up to the expectation that they can afford anything in Vietnam. To live up to this expectation means that these men often deprive themselves of basic necessities in their overseas lives so that they can accumulate in order to consume "like a Viet Kieu" when they visit Vietnam. Some family members

in Vietnam have caught on to the fact that while income dispar-
ities exist between the West and Vietnam, some Viet Kieu
struggle financially to make ends meet in their daily overseas
lives. This knowledge sometimes leads kin members in Vietnam
to prevent Viet Kieu from overspending by, for example, cooking at home rather than taking entire family and kin to eat huge
feasts at restaurants.

For the most part, however, I found that most kin members
in Vietnam attempt to "save face" for all involved, particularly
for the visiting Viet Kieu, by embracing and participating in
small-scale conspicuous consumption when the Viet Kieu visits.
They do so in order to prevent embarrassment for the visiting
Viet Kieu, especially men, since it is men who do most of the
paying in the leisure economy of Vietnam. Family members save
face even when they know that it comes at a tremendous cost
for their overseas loved ones; they, in effect, help the visiting
Viet Kieu garner a sense of self-worth in the public's eyes.

Kin members in Vietnam also benefit materially from Viet
Kieu small-scale conspicuous consumption patterns, which the
Vietnamese kin members often do not want to undermine.
They go through great lengths to commend Viet Kieu for having a "luxurious life in the West," even to the extent of recognizing that Viet Kieu can "burn money." On many occasions,
transpacific husbands confided in me the burden of consumption when they go to Vietnam. Toan recounted numerous
stories of how kin members in Vietnam did not fully understand
that his income in the United States was very low. In one story,
Toan told me of a twenty-something female cousin of his new
wife who, in the presence of over twenty kin members, publicly
asked Toan to buy her a bottle of perfume at a department store
that had just opened up in central Saigon. In her public request,
Toan told me she jokingly said, "A $50 bottle of perfume means
nothing to you, Toan. You can burn money when you visit
here, right?" As Toan described to me, as the noisy and attentive

audience watched for a reply, Toan simply said, "Fifty dollars is nothing [*khong co gi*]."

When I asked what happened afterward, Toan said some family members laughed, some clapped their hands at Toan's reply, and that eventually, but reluctantly, Toan bought the cousin the US$50 bottle of perfume.

"Fifty dollars could buy me several hundred packages of instant noodles," Toan explained, "in Los Angeles."

CHAPTER 3

Globalization as a Gender Strategy

AT ROUGHLY 5 FOOT 5, forty-two-year-old Bao
Hoang was a little out of shape, though not overweight. From
his walk and posture, one can tell that Bao had little leisure time,
and that work, however flexible he claimed it to be, filled most
of his time in Boston. With only a village grade-school education from Vietnam, Bao worked at two low-wage jobs, one
in a nail salon, the other at a flea market. He said he enjoyed
doing both because, unlike many of his low-wage peers with
whom I spoke in this study, he had a lot of contact with people
as well as a higher degree of autonomy than most low-wage
earners. During weekdays, he drove for five minutes in his new
Honda Accord to his workplace, a nail salon in a strip mall col-
ored by countless neon lights, where he cleaned and painted
people's finger and toe nails, usually those of women. He did
this for roughly ten to thirteen hours a day, making on average
$10 an hour, sometimes more with generous tips. Like most
workers in ethnic entrepreneurial economies, he had no medical
benefits and no institutionalized vacation time.

But as is the case in many ethnic enterprises, his employers
were quite flexible about the time that Bao took off from his
"nail work [*lam nail*]." According to Bao, for example, he could
decide to go to Vietnam at any time for months at a time, as
long as he understood that those vacations were unpaid. And
his female boss allowed him to take weekends off in order for

him to operate a business in a small stall at a flea market. Thus, on both days of the weekend, Bao drove about forty-five minutes to an open-air flea market that catered mainly to African Americans, where he sold an assorted odd mix of new, but pirated, merchandise, including handbags, blankets, and belts he bought in bulk from Korean merchants in the Chinatown of New York City.

On a monthly basis, Bao had to make the ten-hour round-trip drive from Boston to New York to purchase inventory, and he usually did the trip in one day. He would take off on Friday afternoons from the nail salon, drive for five hours to New York to meet Korean wholesalers before they closed their shops, and then arrive back in Boston after midnight to rest so that he could open up his stall at the flea market early Saturday morning. The flea market business operated every weekend, rain or snow. He made twice there what he made hourly at the nail salon. At both the nail salon and the flea market, he enjoyed talking and socializing with people, but he liked the nail work more because he got to speak more Vietnamese with his coworkers. This made perfect sense, because in his flea market business and in his monthly drives to New York City, he was most often linguistically alone; most transactions at the flea market were not based on relationships where he actually shared a conversation, but were done as quick civil encounters to sell (Gutek 1995). When I compared my three visits to him at the flea market and at the nail salon, Bao appeared to be more himself, more talkative, and more social at the nail salon. There, he laughed more.

Although he migrated to the United States twenty-two years ago, Bao felt much more connected to the Gio Mua village in Vietnam where he was born and grew up than to the modest one-bedroom apartment in Boston where he had lived since migrating as a boat refugee with several of his siblings. When I met him in February 2001, Bao had been back to

Gio Mua three times to visit his parents, who lived there until 1992, when he and his siblings sponsored them to the United States. He and his parents continued to go back in order to visit other important relatives after their migration, although most of Bao's large network of kin were scattered throughout the United States—including six siblings, all of whom were married, and a total of over forty nieces and nephews. He, three brothers, and one sister lived within two miles of each other in Boston; the last sibling, a sister, had moved to Florida to open up a restaurant with her husband. Like a number of families I met, Bao's parents "rotated," to live with their adult children throughout the year, staying on average two months at each adult child's house. They had never stayed with Bao, however, since he was not married until recently, and in practice, this meant that in Bao's apartment they had no daughter-in-law to do the daily caring work as they had in other households. Bao said that all of his siblings had joked that he would have to compensate for lost time by having their parents live with him for a long period once his wife joined him in the United States. Since Bao had for so long felt guilty for not having supported his elderly parents, who were in their mid-seventies, he agreed with this arrangement and said that "my wife would not mind at all." However, his new wife, who was still in Vietnam at the time that I met him, had other ideas.

Before Bao married, he had often been introduced by various people to single Vietnamese American women, many of whom worked in his current occupation, which tended to be female dominated. He had had ongoing romantic relation-ships, and about ten years ago he even lived with a Vietnamese American woman he met while working at a Vietnamese restau-rant before doing nail work in Boston. This first live-in girl-friend had left an abusive husband, and prior to meeting Bao, she was a single mother of two pre-teenage boys. She herself had become a mother when she was a teenager. "Women like that,"

Bao told me, "you cannot marry. You can play with them, but who can marry them? But I have to tell you the truth that she was a nice woman, really took good care of me, and so I said, it's fine, I can be with her." So if there were gender rules for Vietnamese men, Bao had broken an important one: he had partnered with a single mother. But he was relatively happy with her, if only temporarily, because he felt she took good care of him.

That relationship, however, ended soon after she tried to pressure him into marriage. "She wanted to settle down," he said, "and I agreed at first." But the girlfriend did not agree to Bao's rules. He wanted her to move in with him, and have his parents "rotate" and live with them. According to him, "She refused. And it took us almost a year to decide because I tried to convince her. I told her my parents were old. They needed me to help take care of them. She was afraid of it, and I just left." With this experience, Bao concluded that the "traditional" structure of Vietnamese family erodes when women have economic and social power in household decisions—and he also thought that that had happened to many couples he knew, including his own siblings, two of whom had divorced since migrating with their spouses from Vietnam. He also saw that in his own analysis of the ex-girlfriend who did not want to live with him and his parents. Bao thus postponed marriage in the United States because he had not encountered the sort of gender arrangements he looked for in marriage. "Vietnamese women in the United States," he explained to me, "have become like Americans. They are too independent and they have lost a lot of Vietnamese culture."

During several conversations when Bao reflected on the care he "owed" his parents, he revealed that, for him, one of the most important rules in a Vietnamese family is that adult sons care for their elderly parents. In truth, Bao was partially right. Most elderly parents in historical and contemporary Vietnam could expect to live with their adult sons (Tran 1996). Bao thought that this rule had changed among many families he knew in the United States. But he was eager and determined to put in his share of care for his parents—an act, in his view, that symbolized his Vietnamese cultural and ethnic heritage. A careful look, however, revealed that Bao's view of the family had just as much to do with gender claims as it did ethnic claims, for caring for their parents was one of the ways that many men like Bao "achieved" masculinity. In a world where he had few status shields since he performed nail services to women who were "social betters" (Hochschild 1983), and since he was a nail worker among women, Bao felt that caring for his parents could be a good chance to feel worthy as a man. About a third of all the men in my study were living with their parents prior to their marriage. Of these men, virtually all said that it was "very important" to them that they cared for their parents in the elderly years. Many men I interviewed often arbitrarily, sometimes purposely, claimed ethnic and cultural identity for what in reality were a gender identity and a gender strategy in their orientation to family, marriage, and relationships.

In *The Second Shift*, Arlie Russell Hochschild tells us that there are differences between what people say they believe about their marital roles and how they seem to feel about those roles. Furthermore, what they believe and how they feel may also differ from what they actually do. Hochschild distinguishes between gender ideologies and gender strategies to point out that ideology has to do with how men and women draw on "beliefs about manhood and womanhood, beliefs that are forged in early childhood and thus anchored to deep emotions" (1989, 15). "Gender strategies," on the other hand, refer to people's plans of action and to their emotional preparations for pursuing them. So in Bao's gender ideology, caring for his parents was the responsibility of sons. He wanted to fulfill his responsibility and he had been socialized to do so. But he felt that the prospect of marriage to a Vietnamese American woman would inevitably limit his options to take care of his parents, since he considered Vietnamese American women too "independent." He felt that most were resistant to living in multi-generational households. In fact, he had his own experience with the ex-girlfriend who, according to him, "did not want the responsibility." In his nail salon world, too, Bao told me he met many women who had "refused" to live with their husbands' families. At the same time, he also knew several men who had gone back in recent years to Vietnam for marriage. In his observations, there were good results in those international marriages when the wives migrated to join their husbands. Bao saw the option of an international marriage as a good strategy for family life and for affirming a sense of self-worth. Globalization, then, was his gender strategy when he returned to Vietnam for marriage .

INTERNAL MIGRATION
AND MARRIAGEABILITY

Thu Vo, Bao's wife, was educated in Saigon, and at the time that I met her she had returned to teach grammar school in her home village of Gio Mua, from where Bao originated. Unlike Bao, who had been in the United States for over twenty years, Thu had an unusual command of the English language and pre-ferred to use it in our interviews. She and I effortlessly switched between English and Vietnamese when we met. Thu lived with her parents, her eldest brother, two sisters (one married), and assorted other kin members. When we met in mid-June 2000, Thu wore noticeably more makeup than many women in her social setting, and she was wearing blue jeans as opposed to the *do bo*, the traditional colorful matching silk pants and shirts that most village women wear as they go about their daily lives. We met in a small open-air food stand near the river not too far from her house, and soon after, through subsequent interviews, I became acquainted with her family and their house.

Thu's voice was exceedingly crisp and commanding for someone who stood at barely five feet. Her laughter from afar could easily wake up farmers outside taking their afternoon rest from harvesting rice. A few of these men who knew Thu jokingly told me in passing that one of the reasons why Thu had not been married until the age of thirty-four was because men—including some of them—could not bear her loud and "unfeminine" personality. Most other people I talked to warned that Thu was no longer marriageable in Vietnam, at least not in the village. From Thu's standpoint, she said that she would rather have stayed single than to marry a village man because she felt village men "controlled" their wives. She had two sisters who married locally in Vietnam. She said these two sisters were happy with their marriages because they were "lucky." One married a Canadian Vietnamese, while the other sister lived with her husband in Saigon as a housewife and a dutiful live-in daughter-in-law. Thu said this second sister was lucky because her parents-in-law were generous people and they treated her well.

In the cultural space of the Mekong Delta, Thu had not been able to meet someone who would permit her the autonomy that most village women would *not* expect after marriage. Thu, for example, liked to travel alone with her unmarried friends to Saigon or to other regions of Vietnam for vacations, something she said she probably would not be able to do if she married a local man. In the urban scene of Saigon where she went to college, as she explained to me, she could probably have found a husband who did not want to live with his parents. But like many Vietnamese people who attribute their single status to "bad luck," she said she was unlucky, and that her "numerology [*so phan*]" was circling in the wrong constellation while she spent time in Saigon as a student. Once she returned to the Mekong Delta her marital options were limited—more than when she was in Saigon, because by comparison to the men in

Saigon, the village men she knew were much more traditional in their orientation to marriage and family life.

At first glance, there seemed to be few linkages to the rest of the world in Thu's remote village in the Mekong Delta province of Se Long. For instance, only a third of the households in this village had access to modern plumbing. According to Thu, however, at least seven households in her hamlet of about eighty or so had extensive networks of transnational ties. It was easy to spot them as a group: air-conditioned homes, bright pastel paint on the houses' exteriors, and expensive brand-name motorbikes parked at the front door. Thu's family was one I could spot, and they, predictably, enjoyed remittances. Nonremittance households were easy to distinguish from those with remittances, since the former rarely had air conditioners (with generators placed in the back of their houses) nor were their houses painted in bright pastel colors. If the appearance of their houses was a good measure of how much these families received from remittances, Thu's family's would have ranked somewhere at the top. Inside there was an astonishing antique Vietnamese feel, yet modern appliances decorated various areas, including several televisions, air conditioners in two of the three bedrooms, tiles on the kitchen floor, an electric stove in the kitchen, and tubs in the one of the two bathrooms that I got to visit. Most of these gifts had been bought in Saigon after they were imported from a more developed Asian country like Japan or Hong Kong. In an unusual pattern, the remittances Thu's family received were not technically from abroad, but rather from her Vietnamese-Canadian brother-in-law, Vu, who was living with Thu's family in Gio Mua.

TRANSNATIONAL MATCHMAKING
IN THE LOCALITY OF ORIGIN

Two years before I met Thu, Vu married Thu's younger sister, Chau. After graduating near the top of his class at the University of Toronto, he worked for an engineering company in Canada that produced custom-made plastic bags for retailers all over the world. Like many companies that moved their factories to rural regions of the third world, Vu's company moved to the Mekong Delta, and it transferred Vu to supervise the factory there, an opportunity Vu took after his marriage to Chau was arranged by a family relative while he was living in Canada. Vu said that he preferred to live in Vietnam because it was "exciting," and that it allowed him to become "more Vietnamese," but he would one day want to go back to Canada. "My parents are happy about the arrangement because people here really defer to them when they visit us," explained Vu, as if to apologize for not living with his own parents in Canada. "They [his parents] love to visit because they can afford to do many more things here that they cannot do in Canada." Vu was thus part of a peculiar pattern, by reverse migrating and transgressing traditional Vietnamese family practices to live with his in-laws in Gio Mua rather than with his parents who were living in Canada.

Vu said that he found in his wife's family the sort of closeness that he didn't have growing up in the West. While living with his wife's family, Vu found in his sister-in-law, Thu, many resemblances to a Canadian white female friend with whom he had shared many laughs in college. As he explained, "In Vietnam, it's odd for people, especially adults, to have opposite-sex friends, so it's unusual to tell people about my history with this white female friend I had in college. We were not lovers, just really close as true friends. And I survived college because of her." In Vu's opinion, Thu was funny, articulate, and "She's the kind of person who gets what she wants. I really admire that in a friend. They inspire me." As for Thu, the feelings of being good friends were mutual—she admired Vu because she saw in him a man of respectability, who "does not need to control his wife to be a man." She believed that Vu was truly egalitarian, someone who respected and at times even deferred to his wife.

Vu was committed to "helping Thu find a good husband," as he framed it, not only because he cared for Thu as a friend and as a sister-in-law but also because he saw good things in Bao, someone who he had known through his elder brother ever since he was a young boy. When he was in college, Vu had made frequent trips to New York City from Toronto, where he met up with Bao during Bao's visits to Chinatown to buy merchandise for his flea market business. Vu said his elder brother and Bao had been friends for over twenty years, and Vu admired Bao for his hard work and his sense of commitment to people. Because Thu trusted Vu as a friend and, more important, as a brother-in-law, she trusted that Vu would make good judgments about Bao's suitability. Vu wanted to be sure that Thu was not, as he said, "stuck in Vietnam marrying some poor farmer in the Delta." Vu felt that Bao was probably like him as a man living in the West. Yet at thirty-five, Vu's formative years were in Canada, since he had migrated almost thirty years before with his family, and in many ways he said he was "truly Canadian, truly Western." He was also truly different from Bao. Whereas Vu migrated to the West as a child, Bao migrated in his early adulthood. And whereas Vu was a high-wage professional in the male world of engineers, Bao was a low-wage worker in the feminized world of the nail salon.

Matchmaking as a Transnational Activity

It was most important for Bao, as he repeatedly told me, to put in his share of caring for his elderly parents who were already in their mid-seventies. He had good justification for doing so. "It took them lots of efforts and resources to provide for our siblings to pay for our journeys to the United States," he revealed, like a person yearning to pay off a house mortgage. It was a big debt, but he knew there was an end to it. Indeed, boat refugees needed resources in order to get on those organized boats in the first place, and Bao felt that his debt compounded over time. He felt he had to repay them not only for raising him in Vietnam but also for the gift of migration. But what was most important for Bao was least desirable, if not most fearful, for Thu. She knew she was anomalous when it came to the world of women in the Mekong Delta because she strongly resisted the role of a daughter-in-law. She did not resist because she had a role model, nor did she witness in her social world specific cases of hostility from mothers-in-law. "I just don't like the idea of it," she explained to me, as if she were laying out a speech on feminism. "Vietnam is an odd place because people are still so behind. Women and men should be equal. I just feel that that is the most important way a young woman can be under control of not only her mother-in-law but her husband's entire family. I like to live by myself, to live with my husband only."

To the outsider, then, it may seem preposterous that she married Bao, since she feared living with prospective in-laws. And it also seems preposterous that Bao chose marriage with Thu, since marriage was important to him for that very reason. Did Thu not know about the man she chose to marry? Was Bao unaware of Thu's approach to family and marital life? Or was there a mix-up because Vu was just another bad matchmaker trying to get social recognition, as many matchmakers do? To interpret their peculiar match-up, we need to explicitly understand their "marriageability" over time. This might help us understand the use of globalization as a gender strategy on both sides of the Pacific.

As a low-wage immigrant man who worked in a feminized occupation in the United States, Bao felt he had low marriageability in the Vietnamese American marriage market. "It's common sense that women in America," as he would tell me, "even the women who work with me in the nail salon, are picky about who they marry because I don't make much money." On the other side of the gender line, Thu was priced out of the Mekong

Delta marriage market because she was a teacher with an important public image, which intimidated many Mekong Delta men
of lesser social and economic status. Thu had chosen to reverse
her migration back to Gio Mua after her education in Saigon in
order to live with her parents, but that movement meant that she
ended up with few opportunities to meet men who she saw as
suitable grooms, and who might see her as a suitable bride.
"Some of the men here have never even seen urban life in
Saigon," she explained. "So it's odd to them to see me wearing
different things that I wore when I spent five years in Saigon for
college." One single man I spoke to who knew Thu explained,
"When you marry an urban woman with too many resources,
later on, she will humiliate you if you don't know how to talk to
her, or have enough money to support her. It's best to stay away
from women like Thu."

HISTORIES OF MIGRATION

With their different kinds of migrations over time—Bao's
migration from Gio Mua to the United States, and Thu's migration from Gio Mua to Saigon and back—something funda-
mentally changed about their marriageability. Bao had not yet
entered wage work prior to his migration to the United States
in 1979; he was only twenty at the time, and for most men coming of age in the Delta then and now, life in a rural and repres-
sive economy of the underdeveloped world meant that he was
still living at home. He said he was economically reliant on his
parents, but that prior to his migration to the United States in
1979, his parents were petty merchants who sold hardware in
the marketplace, and so he helped out there a little before he left
Vietnam as a boat refugee. He told me that he had done odd
jobs in Boston prior to entering the nail salon niche about three
years ago, when many Vietnamese were taking on this particular ethnic labor niche. "It's good money," he explained, "but not

glamorous for a man to do. Sometimes I feel embarrassed about telling people that I 'do' nails."

Thu, on the other hand, acquired too much cultural capital, and perhaps too much social worth, once she left the Delta for schooling in Saigon, and upon her return, her cultural capital priced her out of the local marriage market. Both Thu's and Bao's past and present social locations altered their cartographies of desire for a marital partner in circuitous ways (Pflugfelder 1999). What they wanted in a marital partner at the time that I met them they would not be able to find easily in their local space, for they were both facing different forms of social change that they were not able to accept. He was on the receiving end of a change he did not want because Vietnamese American immigrant women were taking on new gender identities and practices as a result of migration to the United States. She was part of a social change in Vietnam, for it was the men in her local context who remained the same in their cultural outlooks on marriage and family life as she took on new meanings and practices to those aspects of life.

Over a decade ago, Nazli Kibria provided what is now the most important contribution to understanding the effects of migration on gender relations among Vietnamese immigrant families. In her case study of the initial years of settlement among Vietnamese refugees in Philadelphia who arrived in the late 1970s and early 1980s, Kibria found that while women and children had ample opportunity to challenge traditional and hegemonic Vietnamese kinship systems, "neither of these previously disenfranchised groups within the family used this opportunity to reject completely the traditional Vietnamese family system." Some women held on to patriarchal traditions after migration because they found that it was one way of mobilizing men to provide for families and to maintain authority over children. Vietnamese American women, Kibria observed, "saw little value in the demise of the traditional family system. For

them, as for many other women in the United States, the fall of
a family order that provided them with economic support was
not something to hasten or even to welcome, given their
economic vulnerability and dependence on family ties"
(1993, 169).

Kibria's important findings have been widely regarded by
scholars as an exception to other empirical studies on postmigration gender relations and experiences in the general immigrant population. For many immigrant women, the migration
process offers new terrains for reorganizing preexisting gender
regimes. I suggest here that over time, the formation of the
Vietnamese diaspora and the transnational linkages with those
"left behind" have created new challenges to gendered transitions (Hondagneu-Sotelo 1994) that generally did not exist at
the time that Kibria conducted her study in the early 1980s. At
the same time, these transitions in overseas communities have a
significant impact on those who stay put in Vietnam. Thus,
transnational ties have created new models among contemporary transnational families in the Vietnamese diaspora. It was Vu,
for example, Thu's brother-in-law, who in large part matched
Bao and Thu, and it was also Vu who made sure they knew the
reality of their marital situations. Because he constantly tra-
versed the Pacific, going back and forth at least four times a year,
Vu gained enormous legitimacy as someone who understood
complex social dynamics in his transnational circuits of the
Mekong Delta and the West. In Vietnam he was seen as truly a
"Westerner" because he grew up in Canada, and in North
America he was seen as an authentic Vietnamese because he
married in Vietnam and had been living there for several years.
He had authority to socially "remit" values and practices across
the diaspora (Levitt 1998), and in both ends of the transnational
social field. He understood the situations of Thu and Bao, and
he understood that in reality, both of them would remain permanently single if they did not go global. "I've lived in the

Mekong Delta for three years now," he explained as if he were about to report a research finding, "and I know that Thu would have a real problem with many of the village men because she's too independent. She's definitely not a typical Vietnamese woman. Bao, on other hand, would have real problems with the women in Boston because he's still stuck on taking care of his parents."

Bao and Thu altered their expectations, but only because they were able to go global in their choice of a marital partner. They spoke of emotional preparations and strategies for possible futures. For Bao, marrying Thu was actually expensive. He initially felt that he could not "afford" the international marriage. Indeed, there are real financial costs to marry transnationally. But Bao also knew that Thu would be "okay" with living with his parents, and unlike some other low wagers in this study, Bao supported his wife's plans to enter wage work, a key explanation for Thu's decision to marry him. Thus, it was different from marrying a Vietnamese American woman who had already formed ideals about work and family, whereas Thu seemingly had not been exposed to that. For Thu, marrying Bao would require that she live with future in-laws, but it also meant that she had the prospect of living in a "modern country," in which she had the opportunity to enter wage work. It was different, therefore, to be an unemployed daughter-in-law in the Mekong Delta than to be an employed one in Boston.

"Vu told me that even when women live with their parents in the United States, they could work, and that gives them more respect in the family because they can help out financially," she revealed. "In Vietnam, if you live with your in-laws, you cannot work because there are no good jobs available here and even if there are good jobs, your in-laws and your husband would not allow you to work." Thu knew this well, as her sister in Saigon had ample opportunities for employment, but was told by her parents-in-law not to work. Over time, Thu felt that she was not contributing financially to her family in the Delta since Vu took up most of that responsibility. Her monthly wage as a teacher in the Mekong Delta was only about one million Vietnamese dongs (US$70). So in reality, her income could not provide for her parents the kind of standard of living they were used to having with Vu's support. Over time, she felt that they saw her as someone who was generally economically useless. While publicly she had respect from fellow villagers who generally earned less than she did as a teacher, in private, she felt peripheral in her family, in large part because two of her sisters had married into wealth, one in Saigon and one with Vu. But neither one of them worked for a wage.

In some ways, Thu felt like the dependent daughter-in-law in her own family. She said her other sister in Saigon had accepted that feeling and was resigned to being a good daughter-in-law and a good wife. As Thu poignantly explained, "When you are my age, and you're living with your family and they're paying for most things, you feel like you're just a guest, like being a daughter-in-law." Thus, it was Vu's persuasion, Thu's sense that there were no suitable local marriage candidates, her conception of gender in her local contexts, and most of all, her sense of being economically peripheral in her own natal family that led her to marry Bao. If Bao felt that caring for his family was a way of achieving masculinity and a sense of self-worth, Thu's decreasing sense of self-worth because she was economically reliant on her family at the age of thirty-four was ultimately the reason she saw an international marriage as a good gender strategy.

CHAPTER 4

The Matchmaker

I MET SIXTY-ONE-YEAR-OLD Mai Nguyen in early April 2001 at the two-bedroom apartment she shared with her brother's family of four in San Francisco's inner city. It was her usual Wednesday off from work at an electronic assembly line in the warehouse district, not too far from the apartment. The master bedroom in the apartment was taken up by her brother and his wife; two high school nephews occupied the living room; and Mai shared the smaller bedroom with an eleven-year-old niece. Besides this spatial arrangement, the paucity of objects and their careless arrangement in the apartment suggested a familiar story of working-class immigrant life: discolored walls, stained old chairs, missing writing desks, and abundant dust on the window blinds.

I arrived at the apartment a week after Mai's nephew-in-law, Trong, introduced us when I visited and interviewed him at his work in March 2001. Thirty-four-year-old Trong had recently married Giao, Mai's twenty-six-year-old niece, who was waiting in Saigon for paperwork to clear so that she could join Trong in San Jose. Giao's mother is Mai's youngest sister, and the only sibling of four who remained in Vietnam while the other three migrated in the early 1980s. I visited Giao and her family many times in the summer of 2000, and learned that while Mai was living in San Francisco, she had established a notable presence in Giao's home in Vietnam because of the numerous gifts and money she had sent to the family. Mai told me she was indebted to her sister, Giao's mother, and that she had been gradually paying off this debt over the past two decades, a process that tells an important dimension of contemporary Vietnamese international marriages.

In this chapter, I depart from telling stories of the married people in international marriages in order to tell the story of Mai, a typical transpacific matchmaker, who Vilna Francine Bashi would call a "key figure" in migration streams, because "this key figure is the reason that networks are formed and maintained, because he or she enables migration and resettlement for dozens if not hundreds of international movers" (2007, 7–8). Personal narratives of matchmakers and the motivations behind their matchmaking tell an important dimension of stories embedded in Vietnamese international marriages. They provide an important clue to understanding the significance of social networks in international marriage migration streams, for, as Bashi argues, immigration is frequently less about the exercise of "individual choices and preferences in making economic change, and more about taking advantage of the chances for change that come about because and only when network members solicit new migrants to fill opportunities available in certain times and spaces" (2007, 5). I begin by noting that the transpacific matchmakers I interviewed, and whose stories I got to know from the international couples they matched, varied a great deal in their personal biographies and their relationships to specific individuals and specific couples in this study. I divide transpacific matchmakers into two social groups: those based in Vietnam and those based in overseas communities. According to interviews with my informants, the latter group, of which Mai was a typical case, made up more than 80 percent [n = 57/69] of all the matchmakers in this study. In other words, most matchmakers of Vietnamese contemporary international marriages were overseas Vietnamese people.

FAMILY OBLIGATIONS ACROSS TIME

At her job, Mai's task was to make sure that every box of electronic parts her company sold to retail buyers across the country was packaged properly before it was sent out; her most important responsibility was to make sure those packages bore the company's slogan stamp on all four sides. On average, she said she inspected about six hundred boxes daily. Her salary in 2001 was about $22,000, and it had not increased by more than 10 percent from the time she began working at the company in 1993. Until recently, she was usually the first in line to submit her name to ask for work on her days off in order to receive overtime pay. Many of her coworkers resented each other for "overworking" the overtime system because such hours were limited, but Mai did not care about relations with coworkers, since the overtime pay was crucial to her version of being a provider to a transnational family—she was the only one of her co-ethnic coworkers who had families in Vietnam. She said that it gave her a full five dollars more per hour than her regular wage. "Five dollars can feed an entire family for a whole day in Saigon," she explained. This observation was significant. She carefully calculated that if she worked overtime three times a month, she could feed her sister's entire family of eight in Vietnam for the whole month.

A rather small woman, even by Vietnamese standards, of roughly 4 foot 7, Mai's size did not impede her from being direct and insistent, two important skills that I suspected made her a good transpacific matchmaker. This was a role she took on when she returned to Vietnam in 1999 for the first time since she had migrated to the United States in 1984. Perhaps because she was an insistent person, when she told stories or expressed opinions Mai had a habit of repeating herself, often paraphrasing what she would say in the prior sentence. "I think it's important that children listen to their parents," she would explain, for example. "Children should listen to their parents because it's very important that they do." This trait would later reveal her as a careful speaker, but one whose carefulness was expressed only out of a need to be recognized. Mai said she often did not get recognized for things she accomplished for others, and it bothered her that her close family members in the United States dismissed the things she did for them as "routine [*hang ngay*]" or "normal [*binh thuong*]." "I sacrificed a lot for my siblings and nieces and nephews in the United States," she made clear. "But they never do anything for me in return." In truth, she sacrificed much more for family members in Vietnam. That made her assessment of the U.S. family a matter of comparison, because social recognition and deference from family members in Vietnam were often much more striking because of the relatively large gifts and money they received from Mai. As I learned, one of the most important gifts Mai felt she gave her family was the arranged marriage for Giao. She spent a considerable amount of energy, time, and some financial resources in order to arrange an international marriage between Trong, who had been her supervisor in the warehouse district for several years, and her Saigonese niece.

A Social History of
the Matchmaker

As a divorced and childless woman in postwar Vietnam, Mai, the eldest of four siblings, lived with her youngest sister in Saigon for over a decade before migrating as a boat refugee in 1984 with her two brothers and their families. The youngest sister, Giao's mother, was left behind because she simply could not afford to pay for a family of eight to take up spaces on boats that took refugees to camps in other parts of Asia. Mai, too, could not afford the journey, but she had agreed, in exchange for her passage, to take on the responsibility of helping her brother's wife care for three children and an infant, who were brought along for the migration journey. After spending time at a refugee camp in Hong Kong, Mai, her two brothers, and their families were initially sponsored by a Catholic church in Tennessee. With the help of a close family friend, one brother later moved to the Tenderloin District of San Francisco, where many impoverished recent Vietnamese immigrants reside. The other brother remained in Tennessee.

Mai initially remained in Tennessee with the second brother because he asked her to stay and take care of his children while he and his wife worked at the regional post office separating mail on the late-night shift. Mai agreed, as she was unemployed, and they paid her $300 a month at that time. In addition, they "gave," as she framed it, her room and board. The arrangement worked well initially, but two years later, Mai moved to San Francisco with the first brother because conflicts arose over the sharing of money with the Tennessee brother's wife. Mai felt that the sister-in-law eventually "asked for too much" for Mai's share of expenses and that over time, the sister-in-law treated Mai like a domestic worker. She also objected to the fact that her brother left all financial decisions to his wife when they first moved to the United States, an arrangement she claimed did not exist when they were living in Vietnam. "My brother had to surrender to his wife when they came to America," she said, as if migration introduced a gender war among Vietnamese migrants. "She took control of everything. He became afraid of her." When she left Tennessee after spending two years with the family, Mai felt she had given much more in exchange for her passage to the United States than she got back from her Tennessee brother and his wife. As she explained to me in tears:

> I took care of those four children like they were mine. It was a very difficult time—I know that I owed my brother for letting me leave Vietnam with his family, but to tell you

the truth, they needed me more than I needed them. When we were in the camps in Hong Kong, I took as many odd jobs as I could in the camp to help feed the children, and I know that they would not have been in better conditions than many of the other children if I were not there. I was a single woman so I did not need much. I gave so much to those children.

In her social and cultural world, Mai felt that her "emotional labor" (Hochschild 1983) as part of her care for her brother's children had not been paid back. In this sense, the emotional currency (Clark 1997) of care she gave was perhaps worth more than the price her brother paid for her passage to the United States. Mai was fully aware of these emotional credits, and not only from what she had given to the brother in Tennessee. For she, too, in her own personal life had owed emotional currencies to others, namely, to her sister in Vietnam, which she felt she had not fully paid off. Her sense of gratitude to her sister in Vietnam was the reference point from which she defined and judged her brother's debt to her, and by extension, her relationship with him and his family.

For a long time prior to earning an income that enabled her to send remittances, Mai felt she had not adequately paid back her sister for supporting her after she divorced in 1973. She began sending about $250 monthly, starting in the early 1990s. And although she felt that she was sending more than the "market rate," compared to what many diasporic families sent to their families in Vietnam, Mai said, "I need to give them more, provide more for my sister's family. If it was not for them, I would have lived on the streets in the 1970s." Thus, since moving to San Francisco more than fifteen years ago, Mai had worked in the electronic assembly line earning minimum wage, consistently working overtime, to send money back to Vietnam.

Emotional Debts across
Time and Space

Scholars have offered important insights into how and why immigrants send money back home: for example, because they need to support children left behind (Hondagneu-Sotelo and Avila 1997; Parrenas 2001b), because they invest in business enterprises (Russell 1986; Sofranko and Idris 1999; Yu 1979), or because remittances offer an important way of generating a sense of social worth and respect in the community of origin (Glick Schiller and Fouron 1998; Goldring 1998; Guarnizo 1992; Smith 1998). Yet we do not know much about immigrants' lives prior to their emigration, experiences that may drive certain kinds of remittances, particularly those that cannot be measured simply by the return of money. We often assume from this body of research that immigrants send money home simply as an altruistic way of helping out, and therefore we know little about how and why some immigrants send remittances in order to return various kinds of debts they owed prior to their migration. This explanatory dimension of money and emotions is the focus of this chapter.

One of the most important insights offered concerning nonmonetary remittances is by Peggy Levitt, who argued that social remittances play crucial roles in transnational family ties. Social remittances, "the ideas, behaviors, identities, and social capital that flow from receiving to sending-country communities" (1998, 927), help shape the continuing ties of transmigrants and the family members they leave behind.

I could describe with my field notes an entire process involved in arranging marriages, including rituals and movements of people, that would tell us a great deal about the role of matchmakers and matchmaking activities across transnational social fields. Indeed, a whole book could cover wedding rituals in Vietnam, and I suspect someone will soon provide details on that topic. I could also describe the variations among transpacific matchmakers as old, young, poor, rich, male or female, and that could tell us more. I could also create typologies of "social types" that could tell us a great deal about variations among matchmakers in relation to processes of international marriage arrangements, and that would also tell us something interesting and important. But this information—demographics, the process of international marriage arrangements, and their typologies—can only tell us so much about the characteristics of matchmakers and matchmaking activities. They do not explain why matchmakers take on the task they do.

When I compared my field notes and interviews, including interviews with family members and extended relatives of grooms and brides who served as matchmakers, I found that to understand matchmakers and matchmaking activities fully, one has to understand the social histories of gratitude among matchmakers and the people for whom they arrange international marriages. A social history of gratitude tells us a lot about individual emotional lives, and in the case of immigrants, it illuminates an important dimension of social remittances. Indeed, it makes sense that the vast majority of transpacific matchmakers come from overseas Vietnamese communities, since they are able to travel back and forth across the Pacific to facilitate arrangements. Though not always, they generally have the revenues to facilitate what could be an expensive process that includes making international phone calls, visiting potential marriage candidates, and sometimes providing funds (especially for brides) to apply for passports, take required medical examinations for visa applications, pay for other miscellaneous expenses associated with international weddings, and facilitate the migration process of brides after couples marry.

It is the circuits of gratitude among Vietnamese transnational family members that help explain the vast majority of matchmaking activities and matchmakers. Matchmaking, therefore, must be seen as a gift in an emotional economy

(Clark 1987, 1997) among Vietnamese transnational families, and such an act of gift giving is embedded in the "here" and "there," but also in the "then" and "now." As Barry Schwartz (1967) has pointed out, the act of gift giving has psychological significance for personal selves and identities. Matchmaking is a gift among those who facilitate a match, and as such, it bears significant meaning for the emotional economy of kin networks spread across the Pacific. By conceiving matchmaking activities as a form of gift giving, I follow arguments made by theorists across the disciplines that gift giving is embedded in social relations having significant symbolic, rather than economic, meanings (Lévi-Strauss 1957; Malinowski 1959) that are embedded in relations of differential social rankings, and that frequently involve imbalanced, rather than equal, reciprocity (Appadurai 1985; Gouldner 1960; Mauss 2000; Simmel 1950).

A Social History of Gratitude

A year before I met Mai in San Francisco, her niece, Giao, began to make relatively good money in Saigon. Giao's daily salary of US$15 as a computer programmer for a multinational corporation was quite high by local standards in Vietnam, a fact that eased some of Mai's remittance burdens and partially prompted her to take one day a week off from work. However, when she began taking Wednesdays off from work, Mai spent a large part of it doing laundry for herself and her brother's three children as a form of compensation for living with them. "To tell you the truth," a phrase she occasionally used in her moments of wanting to confess something, "it's very humiliating to do their laundry. In Vietnam, I would never do that for young people, but I feel that I have to pay them for living here, and the money is not enough, and I don't have other places to live. So I try to help out so they don't complain about me."

To cope with potential "complaints," and to also pay back what she felt was a gift from her San Franciscan brother to let her live with his family after she left the other brother in Tennessee, Mai adopted a strategy of working a "second shift" (Hochschild 1989). Her coping strategy was to do informal household work for her brother's family because she felt she was a burden on them. She said that she would spend time cleaning and doing work around the house rather than relaxing on her days off, but it was an important way, as she said, "to pay off my debt for living with them." While she was cleaning and caring for these children, Mai often compared the nieces and nephews she had in the United States to the ones she knew in Saigon. She also compared the ones in San Francisco to the ones in Tennessee. This framework is a telling one, for it revealed a micro politic of comparison among many immigrants with transnational family members, an unequal comparison anchored in relations of gender, age, and mobility through migration.

As between the nieces and nephews in Tennessee and San Francisco, Mai revealed that "things were fine" in San Francisco, whereas they were not in Tennessee, as the adults consistently had conflicts in the latter and not in the former. Because of that, she could tolerate living in San Francisco, and felt fine with expending her manual and emotional labor for the San Franciscan family. She genuinely loved those nieces and nephews because she did not have children of her own. She also asserted that she loved the ones in Tennessee as well, because she had lived with them for a significant amount of time. But she loved both sets in the United States far less than she loved the ones in Vietnam. When compared internationally, Mai carried enormously more respect among her nieces and nephews in Vietnam, a degree of respect she could not expect from life in the United States. "When I go to Saigon," she proudly explained, "I don't have to even carry my purse, but here I have to do everything for these children. I don't mind doing things for them, but they show me no respect."

Immigrants tend to experience a dramatic degree of difference in life styles and standards of living across transnational social fields, especially those who come from rural places of the third world. New lifestyles and standards of living elevate social worth and respect even among the lowest-wage-earning immigrants because they frequently compare their lifestyles to the ones they had prior to migrating. For some immigrants, as Mary Waters succinctly points out, "their sense of self is tied to the status system in the home country" (1999, 102). That status system is often reworked in complex ways as immigrants take on transnational lives. This explanation is especially applicable to Mai. From her modest origin in a poor district across the Saigon River in the late 1930s, Mai's life had been profoundly reshaped by migration along class and gender lines. Seen locally in San Francisco, she was a just another immigrant woman of color trying to make ends meet on her low wages, giving back what she could to families left behind in her home country. But seen globally, her life was one of incredible social and economic mobility. It was her impoverished origin and her story of mobility through migration that had shaped Mai's strong attachment to the principle of gratitude and gift giving. Her version of upward mobility, facilitated by global migration, was made possible because of the financial resources provided by one of her brothers.

MODEST BEGINNINGS

Born roughly seven years before the August Revolution of 1945, when Vietnam gained independence from French colonialism, Mai had no formal schooling as a child, and as a result, when I met her, she could barely read newspapers in the Vietnamese language. When she was eight, Mai worked informally to help her family buy food. First, she sold candies and cigarettes on the busy streets of Saigon, and later advanced as a street hawker selling cooked rice and food to street laborers.

Mai's mother was a domestic for a wealthy family, and her father was a street barber. Right after "part I" of the Vietnam War ended in 1954, Mai's father betrothed the sixteen-year-old Mai to someone her father felt could adequately provide for her. Her sister, blessed with natural beauty, fell in love and married into a prosperous merchant family. Given few options in life, like many poor girls during her time, Mai said she felt "lucky" at the time that her father arranged her marriage.

She felt lucky that marriage offered economic security, even though her husband was certainly not wealthy by any measure. Marriage offered her economic security, which she did not take lightly, and in some ways it was a good "job." As she explained, "I liked doing house work [cong viec nha], and being helpful to my in laws. I didn't know anything else." As in many arranged marriages, Mai explained that she and her husband "got used to" loving each other, and she felt "lucky" that he was faithful. But by 1972, when she was thirty-two, it became clear that Mai and her husband were not able to have children, a situation that prompted her husband to leave her. With few options in a climate of war, Mai went to live with her sister who, in the previous two decades, had prospered economically. Her sister's in-laws were involved in providing delivery services for companies throughout Vietnam. The economy of urbanized South Vietnam prospered during the war years, largely because of the growth in the service and commercial sectors that were generated by the war itself. When American troops withdrew in 1973, however, the urban economy saw an immediate decline, from which Mai's sister's family suffered severely. It was perhaps during this time of limited resources and deprivation that Mai began to feel a particular debt to her sister who had taken Mai in as an extra boarder after her husband left her. In her own words, Mai described these feelings: "It's more meaningful sometimes when you don't have much, and you give things to people. They never asked me to repay them. But I always felt that I can never repay them enough. I could never pay back their kindness to me when my husband left me."

THE RETURN OF THE GIFT

Almost always, transpacific matchmakers told stories of someone helping them in their lives prior to their migration, usually financially, in order for them to migrate to the United States. Many explained that the act of migration, and sometimes the process of survival in the aftermath of the Vietnam War, was possible only because of assistance from kin members. Few individuals told me that they were able to migrate with resources entirely of their own. Gratitude among transpacific matchmakers, expressed in the gift of arranging an international marriage, explained a large proportion of motivations behind many Vietnamese international marriage arrangements: matchmakers were returning a debt that they still owed many years after their migration. This pattern reveals several characteristics about the relationship between the matchmaker and the married couples.

First, while transpacific matchmakers were usually related to the brides or grooms, they usually owed gratitude to someone related to the bride or groom, but not to the transpacific couples themselves. I found only four cases in which matchmakers were returning a favor directly to the couple (in all cases, they were to brides) by helping to arrange an international marriage. A second characteristic of the relationship of matchmakers to international couples was that while matchmaking as a return of gratitude was unquestionably characterized by some degree of altruism, it was often expressed as a need to reciprocate for gifts given in the past. As Komter and Vallebergh (1997) have noted, gift giving among family members does not always incur gratitude, since giving among family members is often considered an act of altruism. I found, however, that the Vietnamese I interviewed were unusually cautious about owing too much for what people give them, material or otherwise, and generally objected to "deviant" gift givers—those who give too much. And most individuals were extraordinarily uncomfortable with accepting gifts based on altruism. In this way, the Vietnamese and the Vietnamese diaspora strongly adhere to the norm of reciprocity (Gouldner 1960). As Mai expressed her own experience of gratitude in relations to matchmaking:

> I do not like to owe people, especially owing them for their sympathy or their care, and especially for money. I think it is bad luck to let someone do something for you and never return a favor. If you live well, you should always feel grateful for what people do for you, and you should always return debts you owe. I think emotions [*tinh cam*] are harder to repay. But they must be repaid. If you die and are still in debt with money, then you will not have a good after life.

The third and final revealing characteristic about the relationship between matchmakers and international couples was that because individual grooms and brides were not direct recipients of the symbolic meanings of gratitude attached to the process of arranging marriage, they were often unclear about how they could return the gift that matchmakers gave in helping arrange their marriages. This is because Vietnamese marriages rarely involved dowries, and matchmakers have historically not received monetary rewards for their efforts. Conversations with Giao and Trong suggest that the circuits of gratitude—the gratitude Mai owed to Giao's mother and the gratitude that Giao and Trong now owed Mai for being the transpacific matchmaker—often created ambiguous norms of reciprocity for newly married couples. As Trong explained to me:

> Giao's aunt never asked us for anything. She tried very hard to introduce us. She made phone calls to me, invited me to her home and really tried to advertise Giao to me. I am sure she did the same thing for me to Giao—and so we owe her

a lot for being the matchmaker. Without her, I don't think I would trust going to Vietnam to find a wife, since I do not have family there anymore. I wish sometimes we can just easily repay Mai with money—but it's very disrespectful to simply give her money. How much money anyways? So money is out of the question.

I never heard of cases in which Viet Kieu men paid money to transpacific matchmakers. In a few cases, monetary gifts were offered, but most (though not all) were refused by matchmakers based in Vietnam. There was no case in which a diasporic transpacific matchmaker took money as payment, and few received material gifts for their efforts in arranging marriages. Transpacific matchmakers did, however, as Trong's concern suggested, expect other kinds of return, sometimes emotional currencies, and sometimes something that was not always measurable. In circuits of gratitude, when material and emotional exchanges are made, the sociologist Georg Simmel (1996, 47) pointed out that gratitude often consists "not in the return of a gift, but in the consciousness that it cannot be returned, that there is something which places the receiver into a certain permanent position with respect to the giver, and makes him dimly envisage the inner infinity of a relation that can neither be exhausted nor realized by any finite return gift or other activity."

Indeed, a clue to Trong's concern about returning gratitude was given by Mai when I told her that Trong had explained to me that he felt enormously indebted to her, and that he wondered what he could do to repay her.

"They don't have to give me anything," she told me. "I just want them to take care of me when I get older." In her usual habit, she repeated, "They should take care of me."

CHAPTER 5

Money

AT 6:00 A.M., TWENTY-FIVE-YEAR-OLD Thoa Dang was dressed neatly in black slacks and a bright yellow short-sleeve shirt as we conducted our first interview over breakfast in a small drugstore she owned near the central business district of Saigon. Thoa asked during our initial phone conversation for me to arrive early because she said that by 6:30 A.M., some breakfast street vendors sell out their best food for the morning. We met at 6:00 A.M. for the first three interviews at the drugstore, and for the last, we met there at 8:00 P.M. Thoa's choice of time, her work schedule, and the manner in which she organized her day revealed something important about her: she was clearly a highly productive person, one who was direct, efficient, quick, and logical in her action and speech. This, too, was conveyed by the predictability of her clothes. A short and slim woman with red highlights in her black hair, Thoa dressed for each of our four interviews in black slacks and assorted bright-colored blouses, accompanied each time by the same pair of cream high-heeled shoes.

Thoa was the older of two children from a merchant family in Dalat, a mountainous city about 185 miles northeast of Saigon that caters heavily to domestic tourists. Some of her relatives there owned small enterprises in the central market, while her parents operated a small café that profited according to the seasonal flow of tourists. They were far from wealthy, but were no doubt more than middle class in their cultural context. With income from this café, Thoa's parents were comfortably able to send her to Saigon for college. Her younger brother chose not to go, married locally at the age of nineteen, and by twenty-three had two children.

Thoa, by contrast, went to Saigon for schooling when she was a naïve eighteen-year-old, under the tutelage of an older female cousin, whose presence in the city was the only reason that Thoa was able to go there for college in the first place. When she arrived in Saigon, Thoa knew fairly quickly that she would not use an education in her pursuit of social and economic mobility. "In Vietnam," she explained, as we turned to the issue of money and status, "there are not too many opportunities for people with education. It's based on luck and whether or not your family has connections with important people." She was consistently more skeptical about the outcomes of education than most young Saigonese I met. Her skepticism partly explained why she chose, and strongly preferred, self-employment, unlike most of her peers who were vying for the coveted jobs with international companies.

Thoa passed the rigorous university entrance exams and completed a degree in history at Vietnam National University, even though she had decided in her first year that she was bored with it and that she disliked school altogether. "I finished school because I wanted to make my father happy," she explained in a way that conveyed a sense of obligation and a matter of fact, but not resentment to her parents. Thoa chose to study history only because one of her best friends decided to pursue that field. The best friend eventually won a scholarship to attend graduate school in London. Thoa, in contrast, made little use of her history degree. Thoa said she once speculated that her father sent her to Saigon for college in order for her to find a suitable husband from a wealthy family. Her father, she explained, had aspirations for moving down to Saigon, and Thoa's potential marriage to someone there would make that possible. He was born in Dalat, and had once lived and worked in Saigon, but returned to Dalat to take care of his parents. "He really wants to return to Saigon, but he thinks the city is too expensive now to have a good living," she explained.

Thoa revealed that her mother specifically advised her "to take my time in choosing a husband," whereas her father frequently pressured her to find one. Thoa's mother's happiness with her own marriage, mostly because Thoa's father was relatively well off, had taught Thoa that economic stability is crucial for marital stability. Thoa acknowledged that "in Vietnam, men are different now, women have to work," as if she clearly knew her mother married in a time and place—a time and place Thoa was no longer a part of—when women could reasonably expect to rely economically on their husbands. Yet it was both Thoa's father's desire to move south to Saigon and her mother's advice to take her time in choosing a husband that made up what anthropologist Arjun Appadurai refers to as "the work of the imagination as a constitutive feature of modern subjectivity" (1996, 3). For it was the projection of a possible future, a life outside the local and outside the present, that partially helped to form Thoa's decision to marry across the Pacific. But as she began to talk about her aspirations and her social standing relative to her peers, something else was revealed about her transnational decision.

After earning her degree three years prior to our meeting in May 2000, Thoa had the option of working for a local advertising company to proofread galleys before publication, a job that materialized through connections her father had in Saigon. But Thoa said she was the creative kind, and preferred to work with her hands. She explained that she was entrepreneurial, a trait in which she believed she took after her father. Thoa turned down the advertising job and decided to pursue ownership of a drugstore that sells both prescribed medicine and over-the-counter drugs. Her parents were "ok," as she said, with her choice of owning a business rather than working for the corporate world of Saigon. They paid for the start-up of the store as well as the salary of a trained pharmacist in the first year. Thoa handled the business side of the store.

Social Economic Boundaries in Globalization

"I am a successful woman in Saigon," Thoa quickly explained when I asked about how she started her business. "I make much more money than many of my friends who work for international companies." She did not have an office job, a typical marker of success among my informants, because "office jobs" signaled that one ascended into the formal labor market with credentials earned only from universities. Yet Thoa appraised her entrepreneurship as a job that had status in Vietnam, a country where she said people still "pay more attention to how much money you have than what you actually do to make the money." She told me that, on average, she made over $600 a month, profiting most by selling simple Western over-the-counter drugs like Advil or Tylenol. Her earnings were impressive, considering that the average income for a Vietnamese college graduate was somewhere around $100 a month when I met her. Thoa told me that few of her college-educated friends could earn more than US$200 or $300 by working in the corporate world of Saigon. Thoa was evidently keeping track of money makers among her peers. And in so doing, she ranked herself among those of high status.

Thoa's concept of money, and specifically her use of socioeconomic boundaries to mark the social worth of people, tell an important part of her international marital story. A socioeconomic boundary, according to sociologist Michel Lamont, is one of three types of social boundaries individuals draw upon to mark social standing. In her groundbreaking studies of the upper and working classes in France and the United States, Lamont explains that social boundaries, in short, are conceptual distinctions made to categorize objects, people, and practices in order to define and discriminate between "worthy and less worthy persons." Moral boundaries are drawn on the basis of characteristics such as honesty and the work ethic, whereas cultural boundaries are drawn on the basis of education pedigrees, social mannerisms, and tastes regardless of economic power. Socioeconomic boundaries, the third kind of social boundary that Lamont delineates, are drawn on the basis of "people's social position as indicated by their wealth, power, or professional success" (1992, 1, 4).

As Thoa predictably disclosed, money was important to her, and she felt proud that she worked much harder, as measured by the amount of money she earned, than many of her peers in Saigon. "Anyone can get a job in an office," she said, "but it is an easy job that you take if you don't care about money." Thoa said that if she did not make as much money as she did, she could not wear the expensive clothes that she liked. "If you have money, you must spend it," she said. She bragged that she wore expensive clothing and used expensive cosmetics that few of her "office friends" could afford.

On the basis of four formal recorded conversations and during our occasional informal gatherings over eight months that I knew Thoa, I learned that when she talked about money, she usually talked about status. And when she raised the issues of money or status, as she did each time we met, she raised the issue of men. Thoa said it was important for her to marry a man of higher status, a man who had more money than she. "Men should always be more successful than women," she said. "I cannot marry a man who has less money than me. That means he would have less status than me. I would have an uncomfortable feeling." In a country where status is more closely linked to money as opposed to education or cultural and social capital than it may be in other parts of the world, Thoa's conception of status was almost always in reference to money, regardless of how one accumulated it. Never once did she refer to other forms of capital that may offer one the achievement of status (Bourdieu 1984, 1986).

As I probed the issue of money, Thoa told me that she learned from her mother that money defines people in powerful ways. Her grandmother, too, had taught her that having money is important. These two generations of women, unlike Thoa, did not work for a wage—both her mother and grandmother had comfortable lives, but a sort of comfort that no doubt was made possible by marriage. Thoa learned early on from these women that schooling was not all that important for mobility. Thoa said that whenever she visited her grandmother in Dalat, the grandmother always gave her advice about marriage. "If you marry a man with money," her grandmother would tell her, "you do not have to worry much for the rest of your life. At least you have to marry a man who knows how to make money even if he does not have much."

Thoa knew, however, that she could not depend on a man to support her, for in her experiences, young men in Vietnam were no longer fulfilling their end of the patriarchal bargain of being the provider (Kandiyoti 1988). She explained, "Many of the men today make less money than their wives and they still want to control the house. It's funny because they don't know that women are doing better now. Some of my friends would be fine with being a good housewife, but there are actually very few men who can support a family these days." Even if there were a man who could support her financially, Thoa said she was not particularly interested in that gendered arrangement. She was more interested in earning her own money than to rely on a man's support. She believed that by marrying transnationally, she could migrate to the United States and exponentially improve her earning power. As she explained,

> Money is important to me. In the United States, I can make a lot more money than I make here. I could do a lot with that money. You see, in Vietnam, you can never make as much money as someone from America. My cousin in Texas told me that she could make four or five thousand doing nails. I could make much more money than any of my friends here in Vietnam. I could go back here and buy a big house and a nice car and really live nicely. If I just stay here, I will live like this forever, make only $600 every month. I can't buy a big house.

A GOOD MATCH?

The match between Thoa and Hai was seemingly a good one. Like Thoa, twenty-nine-year-old Hai Nguyen aspired to make money, and not necessarily through credentials that schooling offered. Unlike most men in this study, who believed that education was the best, if not only, route one could take to achieve the "American Dream," Hai said he was not "turned on" by people who aspired to be highly educated, and that education was a "waste of time." Hai held a medium-wage job as a receptionist in a mid-sized international standard hotel in urban San Francisco. Hai's wages were medium rather than low like the janitor or the sandwich maker I focused on in chapter 2. Whereas low-wage workers generally earned below $24,000 a year (sometimes less than half that amount), high-wage workers earn more than $40,000. The earnings of medium-wage men were in between, not low relative to all the men, but far from high.[1] Many men like Hai worked in jobs that required a trade, such as electrical repair, which they had to learn in technical school, through apprenticeship on the job, or by advancement from previous lower-wage positions.

Hai began working at the Crowne Hotel as a bellboy eight years before our interviews. He had attended a community college for one semester, but decided to stop going because he saw "no one get out." It was this route of mobility—through advancement from lower-wage jobs—that gave Hai the sense of hope that he could move up in the U.S. economy by toiling with his labor over many years. On our first meeting in March 2001, Hai revealed his income of about $30,000 per year with full benefits and vacation time, a handsome amount compared to the hourly minimum wage with no benefits he had been making eight years earlier. Yet, he made it explicit that it was a "temporary job," that he would eventually own some sort of business when Thoa joined him in the United States, and that he would be wealthy one day. Like Thoa, who often compared herself to others by how much money she made, Hai frequently talked about money when he compared himself to other men. And if Thoa saw money as an important reason to leave Vietnam through marriage, Hai saw the lack of money as an important reason to return for a wife. On more than one occasion, he told me he could not "afford" to marry in the United States. "Marrying a Viet Kieu is too expensive," he explained, "they want too much."

Born in the central Vietnamese city of Danang, Hai was the eldest son in a family of five siblings. His parents, the two youngest siblings, and Hai migrated as boat refugees in 1982, when Hai was ten years old. For five years, they lived in the Silicon Valley with an uncle who helped sponsor them to the United States. Subsequently, they took on government-subsidized housing in the same area. When I met Hai, two brothers were still living in Vietnam. One owned a small restaurant and the other sold household products at the central market in town. Hai began sending remittances to them when he started working full time at the hotel in San Francisco. Those funds helped them finish high school, but neither of them went on to college. Hai explained that on average, he had sent $100 monthly to each of them before they started their shops. "It's not that much money for us," he explained, "but for them, it made a big difference in their lives."

When I probed about where the brothers received funds to start their businesses, Hai revealed that he had sent virtually all of his savings to them when they started out. He said that they would eventually return the money they had borrowed from him, but he had not mentioned it to them since he began to send them money. Hai felt emotionally connected to these brothers, because of the gratitude they owed, and regularly expressed, to him for sending them money. As he explained, "Whenever I go back to Danang, they take really good care of me, make sure that I have everything I need." This connection explained why Hai began to make frequent trips back to Vietnam to visit those two brothers. "In the United States," he told me, "I do not feel connected to my brother and sister who came with me. They think they are better than me because they make more money; they are too Americanized."

Hai and the two siblings in the United States took different paths. His youngest sister excelled in school and became a physician, while the middle brother finished a bachelor's degree in business and took a job as a manager of a drugstore across town. Like his siblings in the United States, Hai believed in opportunities in the American economy, but unlike them, he did not see professional credentials as the only way to move upwardly. He preferred the self-employment route that many immigrants have taken. Because of their divergent paths, for the most part, Hai said he felt relatively estranged [xa la] from the two siblings in the United States. He explained that "they have different kinds of friends and they make much more money than I do, so I don't like to have too much contact with them." Most of Hai's closest friends (all of whom were men) have done little to achieve economic mobility in the U.S. context. None of them was part of a professional circle of doctors, lawyers, and the likes, whereas his siblings, as he explained, "have those kinds of friends." Hai's social circles included semi-truck drivers, restaurant cooks, waiters, and a significant number of men who worked as manicurists in nail salons. The most upwardly mobile man was a mortgage loan officer.

This world was undeniably a world of working-class men. But whereas other low-wage men in this study felt that they had few opportunities for economic mobility in the U.S. economy because of their lack of education, Hai believed in upward mobility because he wanted to pursue self-employment. He aspired to own a business when Thoa joined him in the United States and, knowing a number of successful self-employed relatives, he had hoped to own either a gas station or a dry cleaner, both of which he said would require two people to operate. Hai had family members who he said would help him with capital to start up a gas station or a dry cleaner. Hai felt confident that Thoa "would be fine" with working at a gas station or a laundromat because, as he explained, "she also wants to make a lot of money."

Money as a Master Status

The story of Thoa and Hai illuminates the important role of money in some international marriages. Their global marital story is one of economic motivations from both perspectives. As I interviewed them in different countries prior to Thoa's migration to join Hai in San Francisco, I learned that they had significantly different reasons when it came to explaining how money was important for them to seek an international marriage. Thoa already had a life of comfort and a strong identification with high status among her peers. An international marriage may enhance her ability to acquire exponentially more money through work in the United States, given the global wage divide between Vietnam and the West. A marriage for Hai would enhance his chances for economic mobility through self-employment that he believed could only be possible if he had a wife to help him run a business enterprise. He also knew that his economic status made him less marriageable in the United States, so a transnational one was seemingly the only option. Hers was a story of an economic strategy through marriage, but his was equally a story of an economic strategy, a male one. Money was the "master status" for both Thoa and Hai, and marriage offered the possibility to enhance that status.

Robert Merton (1967) argues that individuals carry a number of different aspects to their identity, but one key or "master" aspect may be used by society to define them. I make the point that individuals may select a master status from a number of different aspects of their identities, for which they want to be identified. For some individuals participating in the Vietnamese global marriage market, money is the master status from which a decision is made about an international marriage. Whereas some scholars have focused on global marital options as one strategy women take to escape poverty (Brennan 2004; Glodava and Onizuka 1994), I found that poverty as a reason for international marriage and international migration applied to only a small proportion of brides in this study. It was the emergent practice of drawing socioeconomic boundaries, rather than to escape poverty, in order to stake claims to social worth and personhood, that formed the basis for many international marriages in the Vietnamese diaspora.

Beneath Hai's understanding of Thoa's desire to make large amounts of money, an understanding that was fairly accurate, was his own gender strategy of finding a wife from Vietnam to help in his economic mobility. The aspiration to move upwardly in the American economy through self-employment offers an important clue to these men's decisions to return to Vietnam for wives. For, like immigrants in the early periods of movement from Asia to America during the mid-nineteenth through early twentieth centuries (Glenn 1983), returning home to marry is an important strategy for forming small producer households with the prospect of the wives' labor after migration. Thoa will move from a preindustrial self, in which she runs her own drugstore and spends her money as she wishes, to a postindustrial life in San Francisco, where she will work in a family enterprise like a laundromat or a gas station. She will have a modern marriage, facilitated by the forces of globalization. But she will face premodern tendencies in that marriage. Her transnational marriage may provide her the route to earn exponentially more money than she was earning in Saigon. But for whom will that money be earned?

CHAPTER 6

The Two Unmarriageables

HOURS BEFORE her husband's plane was due, Thanh Nguyen and about thirty of her family members and kin were anxiously waiting outside of Tan Son Nhat, Saigon's international airport. Like those who look forward to the "homecoming" of a family member or a close friend from the Vietnamese diaspora, Thanh's family was understandably excited on this rainy day in July 2000. For many, the waiting is an event in itself. More often than not, they come to the airport long before the flight's arrival. Since in most developing Asian cities only passengers can wait inside the airport, the commotion created outside by impatient family members made it difficult to follow any one conversation. As I observed and listened like a waiter at a busy restaurant, intently but discreetly, I could make out only fragments of conversations held by people of a culture known for making sure: "Make sure you greet him properly," adults told young children. "Make sure the restaurant knows we are coming," men reminded women. And, of course, "Make sure you always show him love and respect," Thanh's parents reminded their thirty-two-year-old daughter.

The Nguyens were prudent people. For even though they knew Thanh's husband, Minh Do, well—he had made the long journey across the Pacific from his home in Quincy, Washington, three times during the past year—they wanted him to feel welcome and important each time he visited. They had sound reasons for doing so: thirty-seven-year-old Minh revealed to me, in an emotional conversation when I visited him in Quincy, that he often does not feel important and respected in the small suburban town where he lives, ninety miles from Seattle. Seattle is one of the most heavily Vietnamese-populated cities outside of Vietnam, though Quincy itself does not have many Vietnamese residents.

The marriage of Minh and Thanh disrupts what scholars of marriage have long noted about the marriage gradient, an old and nearly universal pattern that women marry older men who earn more money and have more education and, conversely, men marry younger women who earn less money and have less education (Bernard 1972). Couples like Minh and Thanh have globalized and sometimes reversed the marriage gradient. But depending on the measure one uses, it is difficult to tell who is "from below." In demographic marriage-market language, like women worldwide who often find that the pool of marriageable men declines as they move up the educational ladder, Thanh was part of an emerging group of highly educated women in Vietnam who delayed or avoided marriage with local men.

These women found the pool of marriageable men in Vietnam, who were employed and successful relative to them, to be too small. More important, Thanh's status as a highly educated woman made her unmarriageable to many men still influenced by the Asian and Confucian ideologies of hierarchical relations in terms of gender, age, and class. Like highly educated African American women in the United States, women like Thanh in Vietnam were a "surplus" relative to their educated male counterparts. Minh, on the other hand, belonged to a group of surplus men, accumulated in part by the scattering of postwar Vietnamese migration, who were unable to find marriage partners partly because of their current low-wage work status. Some of these men, though certainly not all, experienced tremendous downward mobility as they migrated overseas.

As I have shown, low-wage men like Minh generally worked for hourly wages, though some worked in ethnic enterprises where salaries were negotiated "under the table." For the most part, they worked long hours for low pay. In contrast, women like Thanh came from college-educated backgrounds, which permitted them to work in such occupations as doctors, lawyers, computer programmers, teachers, service-sector workers in foreign companies, and so on. To be sure, not all college-educated women in my study married low-wage working men, and not all low-wage working men married college-educated women.[1] On the basis of interviews with transpacific wives and husbands in my study, I estimate that 55 percent of the couples—thirty-eight of them—involved the two unmarriageables: highly educated women and men in low-wage work.[2] Among all the wives in this study, about 70 percent were highly educated relative to their local peers and about 80 percent of the husbands had low-wage jobs.

Of the fifty-six men who did low-wage work, thirty-eight of them married highly educated women, sixteen married women with high school degrees but no college education, and two married women with only a grade school education. Conversely, in part because not all women worked, I speak of their class status by using education levels. Of the forty-eight women with a college degree, thirty-eight of them married low-wage men, six married men who did medium-wage work (such as jewelry repair, carpentry, etc.) and four of them married high-wage men (such as computer programmers, engineers, and one social worker). Of the eighteen women with a high school degree, sixteen married low-wage working men, none married medium-wage men, and two married men who did high-wage work. Of my entire sample, only three women had no high school education. Two of these women married low-wage working men, and one married a high-wage man who worked as an engineer. This latter anomalous couple is the subject of the next chapter

Unmarriageability is experienced along both gender and class lines. Statistically, because of the Vietnamese double marriage squeeze, there is a surplus of women relative to men in Vietnam and a surplus of Viet Kieu men relative to Viet Kieu women overseas. But their unmarriageability did not end there. If the demography of the double marriage squeeze was a structural condition propelling these international marriages, the cultural belief in the marriage gradient was perhaps a more powerful force driving marriages of the two unmarriageables. Vietnamese women and men in my study had not dared to break the marriage-gradient norm in their local marriage markets.

They believed that by globalizing the marriage gradient, they somehow solved the potential problem of breaking the marriage-gradient norm, since if a man was from a first-world country, he had the "up," while a woman from third-world Vietnam had the "down." It was no surprise that the economic divide between the "first world" and "third world" would penetrate deeply into the private lives of Vietnamese international couples, but it was not always clear who had the third-world life in marriages of the two unmarriageables. Couples like Minh and Thanh—the unmarriageables—exemplified an intense global paradox. On one end of the Vietnamese diaspora, educated women like Thanh believed that a man living overseas in a modern country would respect women more than men still held back by ancient traditions in Vietnam. On the other end of the diaspora, for low-wage working men like Minh, it was partly these ancient traditions that he desired and perceived were still maintained by women in Vietnam. These were the sort of traditions that he believed had been eroded by America's modernity.

THE HIGHLY EDUCATED
BRIDE'S STORY

Twenty years ago, Thanh's father was a math teacher at Le Buon Phong, a prestigious high school in Saigon. After the war, Thanh's uncle, her mother's younger brother, and his family were among the few thousands of Vietnamese who were airlifted out of Vietnam days before April 30, 1975, when Saigon surrendered to North Vietnamese military troops. They eventually settled in Houston, one of the larger Vietnamese enclaves in the United States, and started a successful restaurant business specializing in *pho,* the popular Vietnamese beef noodle soup. Remittances from Thanh's uncle helped her parents open a small candy factory in the late 1980s, and it now has over forty employees. Like members of the "new class" everywhere in the global economy, her parents represented a small but visible percentage of families in Vietnam who enjoyed access to overseas resources, in this case Thanh's uncle and the remittances he sent home.

Thanh was only seven years old when her uncle and his family were airlifted out of Vietnam. She did not recall the political history of the fall of Saigon as well as Minh did, but, unlike contemporary Vietnamese born after the war who would much rather forget about it all and move forward as Vietnam joins the global economy, Thanh was somewhere in the middle. She embraced foreign influences and enjoyed the fact that she had various kinds of access to them. Many of her friends worked in foreign companies as translators or corporate account managers of sales and marketing, and some had become branch supervisors of international corporate offices such as Citibank and IBM. Nevertheless, Thanh was saddened by the hidden injuries her parents faced for accepting remittances from her uncle in Houston. The romantic images of remittanceships between migrants and their communities of origin often ignore the extent to which these remittances simultaneously create both strains and a sense of power and dignity for the sender, and a culture of deference among those on the receiving end. As Thanh observed in her parents' case:

> My father is a very strong man; nobody ever tells him what to do with his life, like how to raise his children. But I think it is very hard for him when he has to deal with my uncle. My uncle is a very nice man, and he cares a lot for our family. But even though he's younger than my mother, his older sister, he doesn't respect my father. He thinks my father has to listen to him about everything, like how to run his business. When he comes back to Vietnam, he always tries to change the ways my dad runs things. And my father always defers to him. He feels that because my uncle helped him financially to open up the candy factory, he has to do everything my uncle says. I know he feels very embarrassed and humiliated inside, but would never tell anyone about it.

Despite the fact that remittanceships create social inequality and stress between givers and receivers, and even greater inequalities between receivers and nonreceivers in the community of origin, it was partly due to a remittance-based upward mobility that Thanh enjoyed the kind of lifestyle she had in Vietnam. After all, the average salary for Saigonese lawyers, according to Thanh, was a little over 2 million Vietnamese dongs (VND), or US$133, a month, whereas the net profit of her father's candy factory averaged close to 900 million VND a year. Thanh earned about 2.5 million VND a month as a part-time lawyer in a small firm that handled legal contracts of all sorts. Although her salary was six times the standard income of the average worker in Saigon, it was still very low on a global scale (Hong, Thanh, and Anh 1996; Nguyen and Hu 1998; Saltz 1995; *Saigon: 20 Years* 1995). The remittance-based upward mobility was of course associated with Thanh's educational and social mobility. It had helped Thanh, her parents' only child, earn not only a good high school education, but also continue to study law and take lessons at international English schools in Saigon.

After graduating from Le Buon Phong High School, Thanh and a small group of her female friends did not choose early marriage, a path that most of their peers took soon after high school. Although Thanh and her friends did want to marry one day, they all wanted to further their schooling. Of her seven close female friends from high school, only one did not go to college. That friend opted for early marriage. The rest, including Thanh, quietly took various professional routes. Most went into fields traditionally reserved for women, including education and nursing. Two went on for higher education. Thanh obtained a law degree, which did not require college as a prerequisite, as in the United States. And the other friend went on to become a prestigious physician at Vinh Bien, a private hospital catering to Saigon's middle class.

Four of the seven, in their early thirties, remained single. Although at the time of this writing, empirical and demographic data on the extent of delayed marriages in Vietnam and across class and educational levels were not available, the pathways of Thanh and her four friends who chose not to marry illustrate a quiet gender movement among highly educated women in Vietnam. These women had opted for single status in a culture where marriage is not only presumed but often coerced. The Vietnamese had begun to engage in a language about marriage and dating that was linked to the intensification of Vietnam's free-market economy. Women and men not yet married at the appropriate age were often dismissively referred to as simply *e,* or unmarketable. In contrast, women (often young and beautiful) and men (often educated and financially secure) who fared well on the marriage market were considered *dat,* or scarce goods. As Thanh explained to me:

> I am already *e* in Vietnam. You know, at thirty-two here, it's hard to find a decent husband. I knew that when I decided to get a good education here that many men would be intimidated by me. But it was important to me to get an education, and I know that for women, marriage is more important. In Asian cultures, but maybe in Vietnam especially, the men do not want their wives to be better than them. I think for me it's harder, too, because my parents are successful here so on the outside [to the outsider] we are very successful.

In truth, Thanh was not completely *e,* for there had been several men who, sometimes with their families, came to propose marriage to her. In contemporary Vietnam, arranging marriage remains common practice, though more so in villages than in urban areas. According to the women and men in my study, as well as available research on Vietnamese families, one of the most significant factors in marriage arrangements is that social class differences between two families could result in difficulties for the young couples (Belanger and Hong 1996; Hirschman and Loi 1996; Kibria 1993; Tran 1991; Wisensale 1999). For women in Vietnam, especially those who are past the socially accepted marriageability age, individual and family success often comes with being unmarriageable. Thanh had several proposals for marriage arrangements when she was in her mid-twenties, before she got her law degree, all from men who wanted to marry down socially and economically. When I interviewed her at age thirty-two and highly educated, she believed that marrying up was no longer an option, as there were few available men in that category. Marrying down was not an appealing choice either, although she had many suitors in that category. Speaking in the marriage gradient mode, Thanh explained:

> When I look up, there are few men "up there" who I could see as suitable husbands. But those men, the few men I know who have more education and who are more success-ful than I am, usually want to marry young, beautiful women. To them, I am now too old. The backward thing about life is that the men below are very unappealing. And of course there are many of them! There are many, many non-quality men I could choose from, but that's what they are—non-quality.

Thanh's marriage procrastination was partially anchored in her confused class and gender status, for her educational and remittance-based upward mobility placed her up one locally, but down one globally. On the one hand if, by tradition, a man is to be "above her," he must be the one to provide economically. But given that she eventually married a low-wage worker, when she migrates to the United States to live with him she may end up being the one to seek economic security through her own means. On the other hand, by traditional Vietnamese culture, Thanh knew her high educational status would not necessarily help her escape gender subordination in marital life in Vietnam, for few men she knew respected women in the everyday context of marriage.

On our third and final interview, Thanh and I walked along the Saigon River early one evening. As the city's buildings rose arrogantly in the background through the din of countless motorcycles, cycles, and taxis, she explained to me, with a disconsolate air:

> In Vietnam, it is hard being single, female, and old. People will criticize and laugh at you. People always ask me, "Where are your husband and children?" And when I think

about that, I realize that I have two choices. I can marry a man in Vietnam who is much less educated and less successful than me who I will have to support and who will likely abuse me emotionally or physically or dominate me in every possible way. Or I can marry a Viet Kieu man. At least Viet Kieu men live in modern countries where they respect women.

Ultimately, Thanh's priority, as an educated woman, in the selection of a marriage partner was for someone to respect her and for a marriage in which a man did not control her, as she observed most men in Vietnam do. As Thanh explained to me: "When I find a nice man 'below' me who I could marry, he wouldn't want to marry me because he's afraid that I'll take control of the house or that if anything goes wrong in the marriage, I could turn to my family for help. Most men in Vietnam want to control their wives, they want their wives to be subordinate even when she is more successful and educated. That leaves me with very few choices in Vietnam, you see, because I for sure don't want a man to take control of me."

THE LOW-WAGE WORKING GROOM'S STORY

In a peculiar and complicated logic of transnational practices, Thanh found a suitable spouse across the Pacific. But if Thanh's desire for respect was prompted by her educational and remittance-based upward mobility, her husband's need for respect was prompted by his migration-based downward mobility. Minh, whose hands, facial expressions, and graying hair made him seem older than his thirty-seven years, was the only member of his family to leave Vietnam during "Wave II" of the boat refugee exodus that took place after the war (Zhou and Bankston 1998). As the eldest son, he held a position of distinction and responsibility for six siblings in a family of educators.

Both of his parents were teachers of philosophy at Le Buon Phong, where they had known Thanh's parents for many years. Three of Minh's sisters were teachers and his two brothers were successful merchants in Saigon.

In 1985, at the age of twenty-one, Minh, then a man of intellectual ambition and curiosity, had just completed his third year of engineering school when his parents asked him if he wanted to go to America. They did not know anyone overseas at the time, but they knew of several people, among the many hundreds of thousands of refugees, who had fled and safely reached a Western country. Minh's parents also knew that as many as half of the refugees on any particular boat trip did not succeed. They died along the way due to starvation, pirate attacks, and often, in the case of women and children, the com-bination of rape and murder en route to a refugee camp. Many were also caught by the Vietnamese government and severely punished with long prison sentences. Nevertheless, his parents were confident that he would make it and have a better life abroad.

In the end, they spent their entire life savings to put him on one of the safest and most reputable boats run by private individuals to leave the Mekong Delta for Western lands of opportunity via refugee camps in Southeast Asia. Like the Underground Railroad established for slave escapes during the American Civil War, details about these refugee boats were kept secret. The boats were made accessible only to wealthy or well-connected families. Being caught by government officials could lead to severe punishment. Many who were not wealthy, such as Minh's family, managed to pool their resources so that one per-son could go, usually a son. They saw this as an investment made with a hope of high returns, as in the case of Minh's family.

When I met Minh, he considered himself "one of the lucky ones." After surviving two years—a lifetime to Minh—in a refugee camp in Malaysia, he was selected in 1987 for entry to the United States. Many people he met at the camp ended up in less desirable places, like Finland, Belgium, or Hungary. As with current migration from Vietnam, the United States was then considered the top destination choice, followed by Canada, France, and Australia. Minh arrived in rural Wyoming under the sponsorship of a local Catholic church. Like many of the churches scattered across the United States that sponsored Indochinese refugees from the late 1970s to the mid-1990s (Zhou and Bankston 1998), his church sponsored only one individual. He spent the first five years of his life in America as the only person of color in a rural town in Wyoming, the name of which he did not even want to remember.

Like many Vietnamese refugees of the past three decades, Minh decided to migrate a second time. He wanted to go to Little Saigon, the most highly concentrated Vietnamese enclave outside of Vietnam, located in a seemingly quiet Los Angeles suburb, though it was plagued by urban problems reported regularly by the media (Leonard and Tran 2000a, 2000b; Marosi and Tran 2000; Paddock and Dizon 1991; Terry 1999). But he had little money and no connections in or around Los Angeles. Then one day, in one of the Vietnamese-produced newspapers in the United States that flourished following the influx of refugees, Minh read about a Chinese restaurant called the Panda Garden that needed dishwashers. Unfortunately, it was not in Los Angeles but in a small town called Quincy, ninety miles from Seattle. Minh heard that Seattle also had many Vietnamese people, and he thought a move there would bring him closer to other refugees.

Eleven years later, at age thirty-seven, Minh still lived in Quincy and worked at the Panda Garden. He was a deep fryer and an assistant cook, which was several steps up from the dishwashing position he was first given. Although to him, an assistant cook carried less stigma than a dishwasher, it was far from the engineering career he had envisaged in his premigration years. His primary responsibilities included making sure the small Chinese restaurant had a constant supply of egg rolls and won tons, and helping the main cook with various kitchen tasks. Though known as one of the best and most authentic ethnic restaurants in town, the Panda mainly served a "white American" clientele who, according to the owners, probably would not know the differences between authentic Chinese food and Swanson frozen dinners.

Quincy was similar to many suburban towns in Middle America—not quite rural, but far from urban. People who lived here drove to Seattle to shop and eat if they had money, but stayed in town if they wanted to see a movie. The town had two Chinese restaurants and a dozen other ethnic restaurants, which, taken as a whole, represented the small pockets of ethnic minorities located in many similar Middle America towns. Quincy also had numerous chain stores that signified the malling of American culture. Minh knew five other Vietnamese people in the town, all men, and three of them worked with him at the restaurant. He shared a modest three-bedroom apartment with the barest of furnishings with these co-workers.

Similar to many Viet Kieu people, Minh is a good example of a giver caught in the irony of a remittanceship. Receivers of remittances enjoy first-world consumption, while their givers often only enjoy it when they go to Vietnam; on returning to a first-world setting, some givers like Minh regressed to a third-world consumption pattern. Like Thanh's family, Minh's family enjoyed remittances, albeit much smaller ones than Thanh's family enjoyed from her uncle. Minh earned approximately $1,400 a month in Quincy and sent $500 of that back to his family. That amount was much higher than the average of $160 the grooms in my study sent to their wives and/or families on a monthly basis. At $900, his remaining budget was below the poverty level anywhere in the United States. But his family had more than enough constant capital from his remittances to keep connected in the small, though conspicuous, circles of families who had overseas kin networks.

And while Minh's family enjoyed their new consumption patterns, Minh found himself lacking the luxury they could afford—most important, the luxury of having the kind of respect he was used to before migration, especially the kind of respect he once had in intimate markets. Minh remembered vividly that in his early twenties, he had been considered a good catch among his peers. He was heading for an engineering career and was from a well-respected family. Recounting stories of masculinity from his early adulthood, Minh told me that young men he knew had not one but several girlfriends at a time, and that it was accepted and celebrated. After all, life after the war was particularly difficult for many families he knew. But he was relatively fortunate, for his parents were well-respected teachers with a small but steady income and, therefore, could afford to spend small amounts of money on leisure activities and materials that bought them some status in their preremittance circles. As he told me in one conversation when we were talking rather loudly, with beers and cigarettes in our hands, in the hot and sizzling kitchen where he worked:

> Life here now is not like life in Vietnam back then. My younger brothers and sisters used to respect me a lot because I was going to college and I was about to get my degree. Many young women I met at the time liked me, too, because I came from a good family and I had status. But now, because I don't have a good job here, people don't pay attention to me. That's the way my life has been since I came to the U.S. And I don't know if I'm lucky or unlucky, but I think it's hard for a [Vietnamese] man to find a wife here if he doesn't make good money. If you have money, everyone will pay attention [to you], but if you don't, you have to live by yourself.

For the most part, that was what Minh had done in the sixteen years since he arrived in the United States. In his social world, Minh believed money can, and often does, buy love, and that if you do not have much of it, "you live by yourself." His yearly income put him just above the poverty level for a single man, but after remittances, his available funds placed him well below the poverty level. The long hours that often accompany low-wage work had also made it particularly difficult for him to meet and court women. If Minh worked long hours for a law firm or a large business corporation, he would get not only financial rewards but also the status and prestige that men often use as a trade-off in marriage markets. If he were a blue-collar white man in Quincy, he could go to church functions, bowling alleys, or bars to meet and court women in the local marriage market. For Minh—a single immigrant man of color—who did low-wage work in a low-status job with long hours in Middle America, the prospect of marriage had been, and remained, low. The pattern of lack of marriage partners for Viet Kieu men extended into other contexts, as well. Men I interviewed who lived in ethnic enclaves such as Little Saigon found it difficult to find marriage partners because, as one man told me, "Viet Kieu women know that there are many of us and few of them!"

As convincing as the lack of marriage partners may sound, numbers tell us that there are still a certain number of women for a certain number of men in the Vietnamese American marriage market. But for low-wage workers like Minh, the experience of migratory downward mobility made it especially difficult to compete on intimate markets. Yet, like highly edu-cated women such as Thanh, men like Minh were on the market for more than just intimacy. They were on it for respect, a sense of respect for marital life which they perceived they could not find in their local marriage market. For men in general, but especially for working-class men, as Lillian Breslow Rubin argues in her compelling studies of working-class families

(1976, 1994), a sense of self is deeply connected to the ability
to provide economically for the family. For low-wage workers
like Minh, the ability to provide, or lack thereof, was sharply
linked to earning respect in marital life. As Minh movingly
explained to me:

> I don't know if other men told you this, but I think the
> main reason why a lot of Viet Kieu men go back to Vietnam
> for a wife is because the women here [Viet Kieu] do not
> respect their husbands if the husbands can not make a lot of
> money. I think that's why there are a lot of Viet Kieu
> women who marry white men, because the white men have
> better jobs than us. Many Viet Kieu women, even though
> they are not attractive and would not be worth much if
> there were a lot of them, would not even look at men like
> me because we can't buy them the fancy house or the nice
> cars. I need my wife to respect me as her husband. If your
> wife doesn't respect you, who will?

And So They Meet

Although Minh was headed for upward mobility in 1985 before
he migrated to the United States, and would have become an
engineer one day if he had remained in Vietnam, he was an
assistant cook when I met him and had spent the bulk of his
adult working life in the confines of a small Chinese restaurant in
Middle America. He had not read a book in recent memory. In
fact, he did not have much to share about what he did generally,
except work, or what he owned, except a used Toyota Tercel he
had recently bought. Meanwhile, Thanh was a relatively successful lawyer in urban Saigon, where Chanel perfume from Paris
and American designer Ann Taylor's shirts were essential compo-
nents of her daily life. Thanh spoke exceptional English, the language we used when she and I met in Vietnam; Minh and I spoke
Vietnamese when I interviewed him in Quincy, Washington.

Thanh was attending an international adult English school to obtain her English proficiency degree, and her reading list included F. Scott Fitzgerald's *The Great Gatsby*. She often prided herself on the fact that she was not as thin as the average woman in Vietnam, nor did she conform to the stereotypical image of Vietnamese women with long, straight black hair. Instead, Thanh had a perm with red highlights and she spent a large part of her leisure time taking aerobics classes at the Saigonese Women's Union, an emerging activity among Saigon's middle class. Pointing to her access to and practice of modernity, she often joked, "Some people in Vietnam think that I'm a Viet Kieu woman."

Minh and Thanh, thus, lived in noticeably different social worlds. But they were united by a network of kin and acquaintanceship that was spatially separated yet held together by the histories, memories, and connections of the prewar years. In 1997, when he was nearing his mid-thirties, Minh's family pressured him through postal letters, phone calls, and, eventually, e-mail to find a suitable wife. Marriage represents an important stage in the life course for most people in the world, but there are global differences in people's sense of time, and in Vietnam, for both men and women, it is believed that that stage should happen long before one turns thirty. In 1997, Minh, at thirty-four, was getting old in the eyes of married Vietnamese people. At twenty-eight, Thanh was considered even older in the female world, and both were old in the Vietnamese world of fertility. Most people expect, and are expected, to have their first child, preferably a son to ensure patrilineal lineage, early in their adulthood. Although the average age of marriage has increased in Vietnam in the past few years, as it has worldwide (Luu and Dung 1995; United Nations 2000), Vietnamese women are often stigmatized and considered unmarriageable as young as age twenty-five. I was told that in village life, some women were considered unmarriageable at twenty.

International marriage arrangements started from different points in the Vietnamese diaspora, depending on transnational networks and class standing; however, arrangements did not always start with individual grooms or brides. Over 55 percent of the grooms I interviewed, as opposed to 27 percent of the brides, said the idea of an international marriage did not occur to them until a close friend or family member encouraged or suggested it. In other words, more brides than grooms expressed an initial desire for an overseas spouse, whereas grooms were somewhat hesitant until encouraged.

The arrangement for Minh and Thanh started when Minh's siblings expressed concerns that their eldest brother appeared lonely and "needed" a wife, though they never asked him. He was the eldest brother and the only sibling not yet married and still childless. The average age of marriage for his three younger sisters was twenty-one and for his two brothers, twenty-four. While the siblings' ages for first marriage seemed lower than the current Vietnamese average of twenty-four years for women and twenty-five years for men (United Nations 2000), they were not unusual since they married in the late 1980s and early 1990s, shortly after Minh had migrated to the United States. His next brother's eldest child was attending her first year at Le Buon Phong High School, a sign to Minh that he was getting old. Minh was often embarrassed when asked "Why didn't you bring your lady friend back to visit us, too?" What his family did not understand on his first few visits back was that long hours of work, as well as the scarcity of Vietnamese women (relative to men) in the United States in general and Quincy in particular, were reasons why the "lady friend generally was too busy to make the trip home *this time.*"

If Minh's choice to return to Vietnam to find a wife was propelled by siblings and then followed by his individual volition, Thanh's entrance into the international marriage market was the complete opposite. Both faced structural and demographic limitations in their local marriage markets, but in different and reversed ways. On the one hand, Minh knew few Vietnamese American women, and those he knew usually earned the same amount of, or more money than, he did, which made him a less attractive marriage candidate in the United States. Research has shown that in the low-wage labor market among Asian Americans, especially in California, women tend to get jobs more easily, work longer hours, and earn more money than men (Espiritu 1999).

In contrast to Minh, Thanh knew many single men in Saigon, but those she knew were far "below" her in educational status and made much less money than she did working as a part-time lawyer and for her father's factory, all of which made her a less attractive marriage candidate in Vietnam. By Vietnamese standards—and for some, by any global standard—women like Thanh came from solidly middle-class backgrounds, through acquired or inherited wealth, educational mobility, or remittances. Yet, while Thanh's education, combined with the income she and her family generated, had not done well for her on the local marriage market, it had trading value on the transpacific marriage market. As Thanh explained to me:

> Any Viet Kieu man can come here to find a wife. And he can surely find a beautiful woman if he wants because there are many beautiful young women willing to marry anyone to go overseas. I think there is something different when you talk about Viet Kieu men coming back here to marry. The women here who marry for money, many of them will marry other foreign men, like Taiwanese and Korean men, but they have sacrificed their lives for their families because they think they can go off to another country and later send money back home. Those men [non–Viet Kieu men] seldom check the family backgrounds of the women they marry, because they don't care. They, the women and the

men, know it's something like prostitution, like selling oneself, even though they have weddings and everything. But it's not really a marriage. If the brides are lucky, their foreign husbands will love them and take care of them. But when it has to do with Vietnamese men, they are more selective. They look for a real marriage. And a marriage that will last forever. And so it's important to them to check everything about the woman they will marry and her background. These men [Viet Kieu men] want a woman who is educated and who comes from an educated family, because that means she comes from a good family. And if her family has money, he knows she just doesn't want to marry him to go overseas because she already has a comfortable life in Vietnam.

News of a split marriage market, one for foreign non–Viet Kieu men and the other for Viet Kieu men who usually have family connections, has circulated extensively throughout the Vietnamese diaspora. Men who wanted "real" marriages were careful to not meet women on their own because so much is left unknown about desires for migration. I wondered throughout my interviews why men were not going back to meet spouses on their own. As I learned when I visited numerous public spaces in Saigon, such as nightclubs, cafés, and bars where overseas Vietnamese men and local women converged, both men and women were fearful of public courtship because of a lack of trust. Fearful that they may be seen as prostitutes, local women in Vietnam who wanted a transpacific spouse rarely allowed themselves to be courted by foreign men in public spaces, as is the case for women in Taiwan, Thailand, Singapore, Malaysia, Hong Kong, and other Asian countries I have visited and learned about.

According to most women and men I talked to in Vietnam, Viet Kieu men often come back and visit local bars and dance clubs in search of "one-night stands" either with prostitutes or nonprostitutes, but they would never marry women they meet in those public spaces. This pattern is supported by my sample of marriages, which yielded only one couple who met through nonkinship introductions or non-arrangements. That couple had met through ads in an international Vietnamese newspaper based in Sydney; 90 percent of the couples had their marriages arranged, and the remaining 9 percent were men who came back to visit and court old school friends and/or neighbors.

If women were fearful of the possibility of being sexually exploited, Viet Kieu men were equally wary of being used as a "bridge" to cross the Pacific by "passport chasers" (Ong 1999). These reasons, as well as the availability of transnational networks, propelled women in Vietnam and overseas Vietnamese men to rely on the old practice of marriage arrangements by family and kin, rather than engaging in individual courtship or the modern practice of choosing a marriage partner in public cultural spaces. Marriage candidates in the Vietnamese diaspora believed that family members make the best judgments in their interests when looking for a spouse. Here, Thanh explained the logic of marriage arrangements that may seem illogical to a foreigner:

> It's very easy to trick people now. Both men and women can trick each other. Women will pretend to love so they can go abroad and men will pretend to love so they can get a one-night relationship. And so that is why people will choose a family member who could investigate both sides for them. Most of the cases I know are similar to mine. Usually a Viet Kieu man says he wants a wife, and then he will call a family here who will search for him. His family member will try to contact friends, neighbors, whoever he can in search of a suitable wife who happens to also be waiting for an overseas man to court her. There's always a lot of

women willing to marry a Viet Kieu man, even though she may never have thought about it until someone asks them. If you have a family member to choose for you, as my uncle helped me get to know my husband, you will end up with a real marriage. Otherwise, it can be risky for both people if they meet each other on their own.

The marriage arrangement between Minh and Thanh was initiated by Minh's parents, who had known Thanh's family for over two decades. Even though Thanh's father taught at Le Buon Phong two decades ago, and was a friend and colleague of Minh's parents, the current consumption gap between the two families had created a social distance over the years. When Minh's siblings convinced him to search for a wife in Vietnam, he was hesitant at first, but later followed their advice when his parents promised that they would invest time and care in finding the most suitable spouse. According to Minh, however, they were surprised to discover that arranging a marriage for a Viet Kieu was more complicated than they had anticipated:

> I thought that it would be easy for them to find someone. I thought all they had to do was mention a few things to their friends, and within days, they could describe a few possible people to me. But my parents told me that they were afraid that women just wanted to use our family to go abroad. We had many people get involved, many people wanted to be matchmakers for the family and added so much anxiety and fear about people's intentions. But the first choice for them was to find a woman from a wealthy family so that they were sure she wasn't just interested in money because if she has money, she would already be comfortable in Vietnam. And it would have been best if she had family in the U.S. already, because we would know that they already have overseas people who help them out so they would not expect to become dependent on us.

In Vietnamese, you know, there is this saying, "when you choose a spouse, you are choosing his/her whole family."

Thanh's family was finally contacted by Minh's parents, a traditional way of arranging marriages in which a groom's parents represent him to propose, often with rituals and a ceremonial language that date back for centuries. Like most brides in my study, Thanh relied on an overseas relative—in this case, Thanh's Houston-based uncle, Tuan—for advice on Minh's economic and social situation in the United States. The family discovered that Minh was a low-wage worker, but a full-time worker nonetheless. During a walk Thanh and I took through the busy Ben Thanh market in the center of Saigon, she revealed that she and her family were already prepared to support a reversed-remittance culture:

> My father and mother didn't care about how much money Minh has. They figured that they could help us out if Minh doesn't do so well; it sounds strange and hard to believe, but my parents said that they could help us open up a business in the U.S. later on if Minh wants us to do that. They liked the idea that he is a hard-working man and that he comes from a good family . . . they know he comes from a good family because he sends money back to his parents. He knows how to take care of them.

As I have discussed, virtually all of the locals I met in Vietnam viewed overseas men as a two-tiered group: the "successful" who succeeded in owning ethnic enterprises or through obtaining an education, and the "indolent" without full-time jobs who were perceived as being welfare-dependent or as participants in underground economies, such as gambling. Most people, however, did not have an explanation for a man like Minh, who is neither lazy nor extremely successful. Thanh's uncle, Tuan, seemed to know more men in Houston who were not only unemployed but also alcoholics and gamblers. Her parents were worried that their daughter was unmarriageable, as there was certainly no shortage of young and younger women in Vietnam for local men her age to marry. In addition, Thanh was already convinced that she was *e*.

All three were concerned that Thanh was facing a permanently single life, for she was getting old by Vietnamese standards. In the back and front of these pre-arrangement thoughts, all three parties—Thanh's uncle, her parents, and herself—saw the option of marrying Minh, a Viet Kieu man, more desirable than marrying a local man in Vietnam. For Thanh's parents, Minh's status as a full-time worker and someone who sent remittances back home to his family translated into making him a potentially suitable husband. He demonstrated a caring culture that Thanh's parents valued. For her uncle, most Viet Kieu single men he knew were part of an underclass of which Minh was not a part since he was working full time, albeit in a low-wage job. For Thanh, Minh's geographical advantage translated into something socially priceless: a man living in a modern country who will respect women.

CLASH OF DREAMS

Highly educated women like Thanh resisted patriarchal arrangements by avoiding marriages with local men. They did not want to "marry down" economically and socially—which seemed to be their only choice with local marriages—because they believed that marrying local men would only constrain them in domestic roles in a male-dominated culture. As Thanh told me, some women would endure the often painful stigma of being single and having no children over the oppression they could face with dominating husbands. For some of these women, the emergence of a transpacific marriage market with Viet Kieu men provided hope for a different kind of marriage, one where they thought their overseas husbands would believe in, and practice, the ideal of gender equity. These women ventured into the transpacific marriage market hoping that their Viet Kieu grooms would work with them to create a much less patriarchal relationship, if not an equal one.

During the groom phase of research, I discovered a disturbing conflict in gender ideology among some of the two unmarriageables—a conflict that neither side brought up to the other. For the migration waiting period was a time for loving, not conflicting. After all, each expensive phone call or visit made was a time to show love for each other, not a time to discuss the seemingly mundane details of what life would be like when the women joined the men abroad. If discussions of postmigration were brought up, according to the men and women, only words of joy about being together in the future were shared. What I found as I interviewed couples in separate countries during this migration period was a clash between the dreams of each side.

Although I did not interview all of the grooms, I did ask all of the brides about their husbands' ideas about gender relations, and about what they envisioned would be the organization and practice of household and family life after they joined their husbands abroad. Among other things, I asked about future plans for household division of labor, whether they would live with or without kin, and women's future plans to participate in wage work. Although these topics make up only a fraction of what we can understand about marriage pitfalls and promises, they provide an important avenue for understanding the interplay and contradictions between a man's gender ideology and a woman's (Hochschild 1989). These aspects are also at the fore of what women like Thanh saw as the sum of a respectful marriage.

From my first interviews with all the brides in Vietnam, I learned that nearly 95 percent of them wanted to work for a wage when they joined their husbands abroad. Though wanting to work outside the home is not the ultimate measure of a modernized woman in Vietnam, it does indicate these women's unwillingness to be confined in the home doing domestic work. Some women who wanted paid jobs were not averse to the idea of doing "second-shift" (household) work as well (Hochschild 1989). However, most of the women, and virtually all of the educated ones—the unmarriageables—wanted, and expected to have, an egalitarian relationship with their husbands.

In general, college-educated women objected to traditional tasks associated with being women, although they did not fully embrace what we might call a peer marriage (Schwartz 1995). For the men and women I interviewed, like mainstream dual-career American couples, marital life goes far beyond household tasks. But these tasks are important symbols in the economy of gratitude among married people, "for how a person wants to identify himself or herself influences what, in the back and forth of a marriage, will seem like a gift and what will not" (Hochschild 1989, 18). As Thanh explained when I asked her about the implications of a purely egalitarian marriage:

> I don't want everything split down fifty-fifty. For example, I like to cook. But it's important for me as a woman of education [educated woman] to not be controlled by my husband. I don't mind cooking for my husband, but I don't want it to be forced on me. That's what the men in Vietnam feel like; they feel that their wives are like their domestic workers. Men in Vietnam never do anything in the house. I think they have to know how to respect educated women.

Women like Thanh wanted a respectful marriage based on principles of gender equality. By these principles, women expected to work for a wage, share in making social and economic decisions for their future households, and have their husbands share in the household division of labor. Above all, they did not want to live in multigenerational households serving as the dutiful daughter-in-law and housewife, the two often inseparable roles historically delegated to women in Vietnam.

Many expressed that reluctance, for they knew numerous Viet Kieu men who lived with their parents or planned to do so in the future when their parents were old. The women's concern about having to live in multigenerational households was anchored in the fact that in Vietnamese culture, and more generally in Asia, elderly parents prefer to, and often do, live with their sons, usually the eldest one. It is their daughters-in-law, the wives of their sons, who do the fundamental daily caring work. Of the grooms in the study, 40 percent of those based in the United States and a third overall lived with their parents, most of whom were elderly and required care. Of all low-wage working men married to highly educated women, about 35 percent resided with their parents. Virtually all of the men in my study who resided with their parents wanted to continue to do so when the wives joined them abroad.

For Minh, a wife's insistence on an equal marriage is one of the gendered anxieties of modernity:

> Vietnamese women, they care for their husbands and they are more traditional. I think non-VN women and Viet Kieu women are too modern. They just want to be equal with their husbands and I don't think that it is the way husband and wife should be. [What do you mean?] I mean that husband and wife should not be equal. The wife should listen to husband most of the time. That is how they will have a happy life together. If the woman tries to be equal they will have problems. . . . I know many Vietnamese men here who abandon their parents because their wives refuse to live with their parents. If my parents were in America, I would definitely plan for them to live with me when they are old. But because they are in Vietnam, they are living with one of my brothers.

Instead of seeking peasant village women or uneducated ones, like white Europeans and Americans who search for wives through commercialized systems of mail-order brides, men like Minh sought a marriage arrangement with an educated woman as part of a careful gender strategy for a perceived future marital stability. As Minh outlined his strategy:

> For me, I want to marry an educated woman because she comes from a good, educated family. It's very hard to find a poor woman or an uneducated woman who comes from an uneducated family, because if they [the family] are uneducated they don't know how to teach their daughters about morals and values. I know many men, Viet Kieu and foreign men, who go to Vietnam to marry beautiful young women, but they don't ask why do those women marry them? Those women only want to use their beauty to go overseas and they will leave their husbands when they get the chance. They can use their beauty to find other men. I would never marry a beautiful girl from a poor, uneducated family. You see, the educated women, they know it's important marry and stay married forever. As they say in Vietnam, "*tran nam hanh phuc* [a hundred years of happiness]." Educated women must protect their family's reputation in Vietnam by having a happy marriage, not end in divorce.

THE INFLATED MARKET OF RESPECT

At first glance, Minh and Thanh seemed as if they were from different social worlds, two worlds accidentally assembled by a complex Vietnamese history. But once closely acquainted with them, I learned that they were amazingly alike. First were the shared social positions of their parents—both educated and middle class. Second, Minh and Thanh were both lonely human faces of globalization, who lacked the emotional and intimate arrangements that adults of their social worlds enjoyed. Most important, it seemed, because of the gendered meanings embedded in their opposite trails of class mobility, they both longed for marital respect, the kind of respect they perceived was scarce in their local marriage markets. From Minh's side of the gender scene, he experienced downward mobility quickly and substantially as a result of migration, and was eager to get back the respect he had lost. Thanh, a woman who had, in part, priced herself out of the local marriage market by acquiring a higher education paid for by a remittance-based upward mobility, wanted a man who would respect her as an equal and as a woman who embraces modernity. He wanted to regain what he saw as something men like him had lost, while she had, in part, challenged the local marriage norm, and in effect, the "control-norm," the kind of control that Minh yearned for in his nostalgia for a Vietnamese preindustrial family life he never had, a life men in Vietnam fully subscribe to and live by. As Minh told me,

> My younger brothers have control over their homes. Their wives help them with their shops selling fabrics in Saigon, but their wives don't make any decisions. I think that if they lived in America, and their wives were working, they would not let my brother make all the decisions in the house . . . and I think that Vietnamese women, when they come to the U.S., they are influenced by a lot of different things, that is why there are a lot of divorces in America.

Men and women like Minh and Thanh had dreams, but their dreams clashed. He wanted the best of tradition and she wanted the best of modernity. He believed the respect he had been searching for did not migrate with him to the United States, but instead was left back safely in Vietnam. She felt that the marital respect she needed was waiting for her in the United States and that she would get it when she migrated there.

CHAPTER 7

The Highly Marriageables

JOE NGO, A THIRTY-SIX-YEAR-OLD software engineer, had changed his name from Cuong when he went to college in the United States because that was when he realized that it bothered him when people had difficulty pronouncing Cuong. The changing of his name was not a racial issue for Joe, for people's mispronunciation of his name was not something he particularly noticed while growing up in the suburbs of the San Francisco Bay Area. As a child, Joe had many white friends, and he said that that "made life easier." Joe was proud that he was able to navigate in the many racial worlds that characterize the Bay Area. Yet, although the multicultural Cuong dated white girls in high school, Joe was more racially exclusive in college. With a nearly perfect American accent that distinguished him from most of the men in my study, Joe had neat model-minority hair, the sort of hair that some men in Asia refer to as 7/3: 70 percent on one side and 30 percent on the other. Just under six feet tall, and clearly above average in size for a Vietnamese man, Joe spoke English with a sense of confidence and properness that I rarely got a chance to hear during the course of pursuing this research project.

On the coffee table in his living room, Joe had a faded picture of his family when Joe was in high school; they included his parents and older brother, Lam, all of whom migrated with Joe to the United States when he was eleven. They were part of the first large cohort of Vietnamese evacuees who left Vietnam days

before the fall of Saigon. Shortly after they arrived in the United
States, Joe's father worked as an accountant while his mother
worked as an instructional assistant for the local school district.
Few of the men in my study had parents with such respectable
postmigration jobs. The jobs most parents of the men in my
study took after migration were usually in the secondary or
enclave labor market, that is, jobs in the service sector with relatively low pay. Because his father had a middle-class job, Joe
explained, his parents had high expectations for him and his
brother. And the two young men met those expectations by
attending the local University of California campus. Both
majored in electrical engineering, and they were both active in
the Vietnamese Student Association.

Unlike his brother, who met his wife in the VSA club, Joe
was somewhat disillusioned with the ethnic organization, and he
eventually worked his way out of the club. He said he initially
ran for leadership positions, but often did not like the cliques
that formed. "Most of them," Joe said, "were interested in looking pretty and wearing nice clothes." Joe was turned off by what
he described as the "matcrial performances" that many of his
Vietnamese peers participated in and after two years in the club,
Joe ended his membership. When I asked if there were gendered
patterns in performances of material differences, Joe explained:

> Of course, the women were especially materialistic. They
> wanted boyfriends who they could brag about, and the guys
> would spend all their money to get a trophy girlfriend. It
> was all a game of good looks and spending, and I knew
> many other Vietnamese students who did not join because
> of that. You can say that it was a marriage market for many
> of those people, but I did not like it. I did not like to com-
> pete with people and date girls who cared only if a guy
> could spend all of his financial aid package in one week. It
> was stupid.

This did not mean that Joe was not interested in meeting Vietnamese American women at his university, but he avoided those in the ethnic club, a place where students celebrated history and culture, but which Joe felt was too pretentious. Yet Joe was conscientious about maintaining his sense of being Vietnamese, while embracing the middle-class privilege that he seemed to identify with while growing up. For example, he proudly spoke about his love for music produced by Vietnamese American singers living in Southern California like Huong Lan and The Son, two well-known performers in overseas Vietnamese communities. Yet when he spoke of his childhood in the United States, he evoked his middle-class background, and by extension, did not talk much about the migration experience, an experience marked, at least initially, by poverty for most Vietnamese refugees regardless of what background they came from in Vietnam. "My parents were involved in the PTA and my brother and I did everything our white friends did," he said, as if to demonstrate his family's exceptionalism in the refugee experience. Often, as with other studies done on adult children of immigrants (Kibria 2002; Pyke 2000), men like Joe in my study referred to whiteness as middle class and vice versa, and instances of parents participating in their school life were markers of being middle class. Such men viewed white "mainstream" families, particularly in TV sitcoms (Pyke 2000), as emblematic of middle-class life. And it was sometimes, though rarely, class privilege, that made up for racial marginality among some of my informants.

Joe was proud of his role-model middle-class family—two parents and a good brother—who he said "all worked hard." For him, as it is the case for many young adult children of immigrants, the family is a place where "normative structures" of American life are enacted (Pyke 2000). Pride in his family meant that Joe had transplanted some of those normative structures— such as a nuclear family, middle-class status, and the American

Dream ideology—into his personal life. Joe recalled how his parents defied stereotypes of Asian people as not being publicly affectionate. He said that his parents were "emotionally healthy" and often displayed their love for each other in front of him and his brother. Joe also evoked nostalgia of his nuclear family. He said they were protected from the pressures of pooling resources that he had heard many other Vietnamese families experienced, since his family had no extended relatives around. And when I inquired about the gender practices between his parents, particularly how they divided household chores when he was growing up, Joe said he was proud of his mother. "She never complained."

Unlike most early waves of Vietnamese refugees, who relied on public assistance regardless of their social class, Joe's parents were employed in good jobs that enabled them almost immediately to buy a house not too far from San Francisco, where Joe and his brother attended good public schools. Even though both of his parents worked, Joe recognized that his mother did the bulk of household labor. She also took responsibilities for Joe and Lam's schooling. The fact that this setup "worked" for Joe's parents led him to associate it with a Vietnamese ethnic model that he felt many of his friends' families lacked, especially those who came from "broken" homes. "Most of the friends I had who come from divorced families," he said, "were people whose parents fought because their mothers were resentful about their roles [*phan*] as mothers." Joe saw a good figure in his father, someone who peacefully commanded authority over the family. He recalled that his brother and he gave great respect to his father:

> Both of my parents are good people. They worked hard. My mother never complained about being a mother. And my father was always in control, but not mean about it. He knew that it was important for him to be in charge of the

house, to make sure that my brother and I listened to him. And if we were to listen to him, my mother had to make sure that she also showed him respect as the man of the house. I admired him for that. That he never made life difficult for my mother, I think mostly because my mother just never complained. That makes life very easy on children, you know.

Joe said that prior to being married, he was concerned about stability in family life. He drew on his ethnic identification to critique mainstream America's practice of individualism in the context of family and kinship, a practice he felt could cause problems in the family. Joe also felt his middle-class background was central to his sense of self. "I think that success and a good life means that a man is able to financially support his wife and children. If you can't support a family as a man, you should not get married," Joe explained. Middle-class life for Joe also meant that a husband and wife are able to divide neatly what is traditionally thought of as "women's work" and "men's work." To assert masculinity, Joe needed to feel that he could easily support his family, and if he could not, then he had not attained middle-class life. As an immigrant child and a child of immigrants, Joe lived in the context of traditional gender arrangements that he saw his parents lived by, despite the fact that his mother worked. Because his father enjoyed the label of being the "provider," even as his mother also contributed to that role, Joe did not see the social costs to men and women—both physical and psychological—as men seek to take on the provider role (Farrell 1975). Thus, Joe aspired to be the provider and he said he yearned for a life that his father enjoyed: two sons with a wife whose work did not interfere with her role at home.

When Joe entered college and subsequently thought about marriage, he was caught in a gender, class, and ethnic paradox: he was in a marriage market in search of Vietnamese women where most women were receiving an education so they could work, so as to become part of providing for family life. Had he sought a blue-collar occupation like some of his friends from high school, he might have been able to find a marriage partner who would be happy with staying at home. "If I met a woman with a horrible job, she would definitely want to be a house-wife," Joe explained. Because Joe went to a prestigious univer-sity, he had few outlets to meet young women who had prospects of having "horrible jobs," or who did not want to work, or who did not go to school in order to work. "I think it is hard to find someone like my mother," Joe said. "She took good care of her children and she worked and it was no problem."

But the *problem* was that Joe wanted to marry a Vietnamese woman (of which there were a limited number, in part, because many Joe knew dated white men) who shared in his conception of family and marriage. His conception of a good family and a good marriage involved a man doing paid work, and a woman "taking care of the house." Most of the women he knew in col-lege were children of immigrants whose parents worked hard in low-wage jobs to earn their way up in order to send their chil-dren to college. Joe acknowledged that few people he knew, women or men, were as lucky as he was. "Most of my friends had parents who worked very hard while they were growing up, worked in minimal wage jobs for very long hours. So I think most people I know saw college as truly a way to move up." Yet Joe was hopeful that he would find a woman in college he would marry and who might or might not work, but who would be happy with her role as a housewife, too.

After graduation in the late 1980s, such a woman never entered Joe's life. His excuse was that the university he attended had too many overachievers. "They all wanted to be superstars," he said. "And most of them wanted to get the best job possible which meant that they had to work really long hours." Joe was no exception. His electrical engineering degree earned him a nice job at a start-up company not too far from the university he had attended, and at the age of twenty-five, he bought a house near his parents. After the house purchase, Joe's parents pressured him to "acquire" a wife and some children to fill the house.

The Politics of Kinship in Marital Choice

Shortly after he bought his house in 1990, Joe and his mother took their first trip back to An Hoi, the Mekong Delta village they had left fifteen years earlier for a life that they had admittedly achieved in the United States. For Joe's mother, Mrs. Bui,[1] bringing home her youngest educated son was an opportunity to display the success for which she and her husband had taken the risk of migration. Many Vietnamese immigrants I met throughout various corners of the diaspora, particularly in Europe, Australia, and the United States, delay the trip back to the homeland because they did not have the material or the symbolic capital to show for their migration. In some ways, migration is like a contest. Losers are those who do not have the material evidence to show that they competed well in the migration game. As Mrs. Bui explained to me when Joe took me to his parents' house one day:

> That's how you should live if you left Vietnam, like my sons. They worked hard and they got a good education at a very good university. There are too many men their age who have nothing to show for their trip. They should have just stayed in Vietnam. They wasted a space that many hard-working men in Vietnam would die to have. You know in Vietnam, if you go back to visit, you really have to have something to show like a big house or you have to have children who were educated well. We are lucky. We worked

hard and my children have good jobs. We have what we came to America for.

On the first trip back to their hometown in Vietnam, neither Mrs. Bui nor Joe intended to look for a potential marriage partner for Joe. "We joked about it," Joe said, "but I never considered it seriously the first time. It was just talk for fun [*noi cho vui*]." Thus, the trip was simply to be among the first groups of Viet Kieu to return home to their village after many years of migration. Mrs. Bui said she knew about the discourse that circulated throughout overseas Vietnamese communities about the danger of international marriages between Viet Kieu men and women in Vietnam, in particular the reputation of "bad girls" who just wanted to have a good life abroad.[2] Yet she believed that if done carefully, international arranged marriages can "succeed [*thanh cong*]." She explained, as if to also warn me:

> You really have to be careful, you know. Vietnam is very poor, and everyone wants to leave the country if they can. Many of these young Viet Kieu men do not know that those young girls in Vietnam only want to marry them for money or the chance to go to the United States. They might love each other for a time period, or they can pretend to love, but it can always change. If they discover that their husbands cannot afford to buy them this and that, they will leave the husbands very soon.

Because Joe had the ability to fulfill the provider role, to buy "this and that," Mrs. Bui had confidence, as she said, that "Joe's wife would not go anywhere." This reflected the usual first thought that many families in bride-receiving communities expressed to me, the fear that "passport chasers" would leave men once they migrated abroad. Some families looked into the bride's "credentials," that is to say, her family's background, to make sure she was not simply using marriage as a bridge to a Viet Kieu community. A few people, like Mrs. Bui, relied on their son's ability to provide in order to secure a stable marriage. But aside from her confidence in Joe's ability to "afford" a stable marriage, Mrs. Bui also had a special affinity for her new daughter-in-law, My-Xuan Quoc. Mrs. Bui was the key person in arranging the international marriage for Joe, as he told me, "my mother fell in love with My-Xuan first."

At nearly sixty years old, Mrs. Bui came of age in An Hoi in postcolonial and prewar Vietnam. She was from a poor family and was married off to the son of a wealthy farmer in a neighboring village. Her father was a teacher of French, and his education combined with her good looks gave them the currency to compete for her husband, someone who came from the prewar propertied class. From her own experience, Mrs. Bui believed in arranged marriage, as she agreed to her own and saw good things in it. "It takes away a lot of thinking for young people," she said. "Older people know what their children need."

Indeed, Mrs. Bui knew, if only from her own arranged marriage, what a man needs to be successful and what it takes to make a family harmonious: a wife who "bargains" with patriarchy by exchanging submissiveness for economic protection (Kandiyoti 1988). For Mrs. Bui, just as for the women in Nazli Kibria's study (1993) of new Vietnamese refugees, preserving traditional gender arrangements ensured male economic protection. Mrs. Bui felt she got what she bargained for in her marriage, and her traditional family system gave her the status to exercise considerable authority over her two sons. So if, in the eyes of Joe, their family setup "worked" for his parents, in the eyes of Mrs. Bui, it was "necessary" for her children. And in Mrs. Bui's world of two sons, where the idea of feminism or *thuyet nam nu binh quyen* did not exist in her vocabulary, she was not impressed by women with an education. "You know the Vietnamese phrase *trai tai gai sac* [boy success, girl beauty]? It means that a girl does not need to be successful, she needs to be beautiful and she needs to be a good wife."

MOMENT OF ENCOUNTER

When Mrs. Bui held a celebration for her and Joe's homecoming in An Hoi, a socially required event for Viet Kieu returning home for the first time, she instantly "fell in love" with Joe's wife. "She was proper, a very polite girl," Mrs. Bui explained. "She reminded me of when I was a young single woman, quiet, spoke well, but very considerate of older people." And if twenty-four-year-old My-Xuan had competed for a daughter-in-lawship in An Hoi, she probably would have been highly ranked. Although she did not have any formal college education, My-Xuan respectably finished eleventh grade in the provincial high school, a marker of being at least "good enough," if not excellent, in the Vietnamese village world of educational mobility for women. And in the same line of logic, many villagers told me, "girls don't need too much education or they will become unmarriageable." My-Xuan was thus highly marriageable not only because she had limited education but also because she was blessed with attractive features, the least of which was long, dark, and straight black hair that exemplified popular conceptions of Vietnamese beauty.

My-Xuan had never thought much about going abroad until she was proposed for marriage by Joe and his mother. This made sense because My-Xuan did not have much contact with the overseas world. All of her immediate relatives were in Vietnam. One cousin, who she said she was not particularly close to, was living and working in building construction in Korea. When I asked My-Xuan why she delayed marriage, because, after all, twenty-four was considered beyond the marriageable age in village life, she explained that her parents had not "approved" of anyone:

> My father has high expectations. He is a rather difficult
> man, and he told me that I could not find a boyfriend
> because he and my mother would try to find a husband for

me. Because my father has many friends and he does business often in the city, he said that I could trust him to find a suitable groom for me. [Did you believe he could?] I think my father could, probably better than I can. My parents are really smart people, especially my father. He knows how to be diplomatic and he has a lot of contact people.

My-Xuan was an "obedient daughter"—apparently a declining population even in villages, according to some of the older village people I spoke to. As Vietnam continues to rely on the West and on overseas capital, many locals place the "feminine subject" under moral surveillance, and young rural women who embrace overseas opportunities like taking English classes, engaging in advanced education, or making friends with Viet Kieu and Westerners easily become objects of critique. And those who maintain the traditional inscriptions of the "authentic" Vietnamese female subject celebrate this ideal as a reminder that not all of Vietnam had been abducted by the West. Thus, My-Xuan was a celebrated figure in the eyes of fellow villagers and her parents. My-Xuan, according to Mrs. Bui, embodied all that the true Vietnamese woman should be. She had long, straight, black hair, and she regularly wore *do bo*, the Vietnamese colorful matching blouse and trousers that the younger generations are beginning to see—and reject—as emblematic of a Vietnamese past. Desires of the present mean that members of the younger generation, both men and women, are now opting for commodities of the West, in part because notions of "cool," which are critiqued by the older generation, have also arrived on the scene, all symbolizing a new, modern Vietnam.

My-Xuan offered a striking contrast to most of the women in my study, because she had a strong identification with being an "authentic" Vietnamese woman, a label that rendered her traditional, and thereby, *hien*, a Vietnamese word used to describe gentle people. For wives and daughters, it often means that they are submissive. "My-Xuan is very *hien*," as Mrs. Bui emphasized to me. "I have never seen her talk loudly, she always uses the right term to address me, and she never speaks out of turn. I know many of the villagers around there who said that she does whatever older people ask her to do. She respects and listens to older people."

Listening to and respecting people were two everyday activities that My-Xuan had done well all her life. As the middle daughter (she had one older brother and one younger sister), My-Xuan always deferred first to her father, then to her older brother and mother in the decisions they made concerning her life. And when I spoke to neighbors in An Hoi about My-Xuan, they almost always referred to her as *dung la con gai Vietnam* [truly a Vietnamese girl]. This echoed the "listen and respect" repertoire that is often expected of Vietnamese women. The identification of an imagined feminine authenticity, organized by family, fellow villagers, and recent overseas actors, had normalized the gendered vision that My-Xuan managed for herself and her role as a daughter, wife, and daughter-in-law. So when I asked My-Xuan how she felt about her recent decision to marry a Viet Kieu, she abstractly explained: "In Vietnam, a duty of a woman is to care for her family and her husband. She has to respect her parents and husband and her husband's family. If a woman wants happiness, she has to listen to her husband and her family. For me, my duty is to listen to my husband and to respect my husband."

Although she considered her family's financial situation as "just enough," compared to many families in the provincial capital of Se Long, My-Xuan's family was probably living somewhere near the "middle" class in their cultural context. Her father, Mr. Thong, had a position in the local government in the district [*huyen*] where they lived, serving on several councils that made decisions about such things as when a foreign company could move a factory into district boundaries. This meant, according to My-Xuan, that her father commanded a lot of respect in public life. "Sometimes, he could earn 'gift' money from people to get their permits approved quickly," she said. Her mother ran a small shop selling watches in the provincial capital, a thirty-minute motorcycle ride from their house. Despite having no overseas remittances, with local incomes from two people and many years of savings, they were able to buy a fairly descent house with some of the amenities that were usually only found in remittance-receiving homes.

My-Xuan's father's level of public respect had a lot to do with how My-Xuan got to know Mrs. Bui, and Mrs. Bui's subsequent encouragement for Joe to marry My-Xuan. When Mrs. Bui and Joe held their homecoming celebration back in Vietnam, My-Xuan's parents were invited, along with many other relatives that Joe did not recall knowing. At the celebration, according to Joe and Mrs. Bui, where there were over one hundred guests, My-Xuan's father had been highlighted as a key village leader, someone who virtually everyone held in high esteem. His reputation was followed by an impressive meeting with Mrs. Bui and Joe, which Joe described: "Everyone told us we had to meet him, that he was fair, smart, and a very respectable person. We felt special that he genuinely welcomed us home . . . he never talked badly about Viet Kieu as everyone had something bad to say about Viet Kieu being stuck up, and he did not talk about money, which everyone seemed to ask about."

The fact that money was never a topic of conversations between Mrs. Bui and Mr. Thong served as a compelling confirmation to Mrs. Bui that Mr. Thong was a person of respectability. "In Vietnam, everything is about money." For many Viet Kieu, the subject of money, especially the explicit request to remit after the initial visit, is a common source of dispute with the very families they visit. Often, relationships tragically disintegrate or simply end when expectations are too high or too unreasonable for Viet Kieu to fulfill. Some people in Vietnam claim that Viet Kieu have "forgotten" their familial obligations and those who do not remit or fail to remit sufficiently are often socially indicted for having "lost" their culture. Those who remit sufficiently are often called *chính cong* or "real" Viet Kieu.

If there is a "realness" that characterizes Viet Kieu, then there is a Vietnamese "realness" that Viet Kieu search for themselves when they go to Vietnam on their visits. For Mrs. Bui, authentic Vietnamese was clearly in My-Xuan's family, not only because My-Xuan represented authentic Vietnamese femininity but also because her father knew how, according to Mrs. Bui, "to respect those from overseas." Respect for those in Vietnam means that Viet Kieu fulfill their obligation of kinship by remitting, while respect for Viet Kieu means that local Vietnamese do not make the topic of money explicit. For Viet Kieu, gift giving is done without explicit requests. For the Vietnamese, Viet Kieu need to be "reminded."

But, Mrs. Bui explained, "When they talk about money, it is to demand." Mrs. Bui admired Mr. Thong not only because of the respect he had from her relatives and former fellow villagers (which included one sister) but also because Mr. Thong had an honorable presentation of a Vietnamese self: he never talked about money. Her judgment of Mr. Thong combined with a particular identification and affinity for My-Xuan led her to propose marriage for Joe, for which Mr. Thong agreed after he had *dieu tra* or "investigated" Mrs. Bui's background.

Like many overseas Vietnamese who return, especially to small villages that often remain unchanged over many years, Mrs. Bui eventually connected a past to her present. Mr. Thong had been a neighborhood friend of one of Mrs. Bui's male cousins in the 1960s when they were young men coming of age during the war. Mrs. Bui learned that the two families' history went as far back as the 1940s, when Mr. Thong's father and

Mrs. Bui's father were fellow landowners. This history marked a peculiar nostalgia for Mrs. Bui, and she helped to persuade Joe to agree to marriage with My-Xuan. The marriage of Joe and My-Xuan was a way for Mrs. Bui to reclaim a geographical identity, an identity that she had left behind more than twenty-five years before. Her support of patriarchy because it "worked" for her and her children, combined with an absence of feminist consciousness in My-Xuan, will ensure that Joe's marriage will not include "complaints."

The marriage Joe entered was anomalous and will most likely "work" for him because, in contrast to most of the women in my sample, his wife had not entered the quiet feminist movement in Vietnam among women who resisted local marriages, the main reason that, unlike My-Xuan, most of the women in my sample opted for an international marriage with Viet Kieu men. Unlike most women in this study, My-Xuan participated in the Vietnamese transpacific marriage market because of traditions of familial piety. She "listened" to her father's encouragement and that of other adults who she came to respect, including Mrs. Bui and numerous other villagers who urged her that Joe was "the most suitable groom" she could ever marry. She was not particularly drawn by the potential material advantage of marrying an overseas man, but she knew that it would immensely help her family. "I want to help my family in the future," My-Xuan explained. "Even though we are not poor, we should always aspire to be better." And while mobility in her family had never come from remittances, their marriage to a high-wage overseas family meant that they had a bright future to anticipate. "If you have children overseas," as Mr. Thong explained to me in a polite, yet matter-of-fact, demeanor, "they have to help their families."

CONCLUSION

For Better or For Worse

THIS BOOK FOCUSES ON social processes involved in international marriage migration, adding to recent scholarly efforts that inquire into the more personal and emotional side of transnational life. As Povinelli and Chauncey remind us, "A troubling aspect of the literature on globalization is its tendency to read social life off external social forms—flows, circuits, circulations of people, capital, and culture—without any model of subjective mediation" (1999, 445). In an effort to remedy this, I follow Max Weber's (1978) mandate that to recognize social action, we must examine meanings people attach to their behaviors and experience. By focusing on social meanings in contemporary Vietnamese international marriages, this book attempts to achieve three goals. The first is to underscore the personal, intimate, and familial dimensions of globalization by grounding the often abstract assertions that are being made by scholars of globalization in particular cases. The second is to consider simultaneously the cultural struggles and material contradictions in globalization by taking a serious look at issues of intimacy, marriage, family, and human relations. And finally, while recognizing the proliferation and usefulness of studies on the overseas Vietnamese as refugees over the past three decades, the third goal of this book is to disengage from the refugee model, highlighting the complex ways in which Vietnamese people in the diaspora have evolved from the categories of refugees to immigrants to transmigrants over the past three decades.

Grounded on the question of convertibility and a theory of transnational social field, I have shown how international marriages allow men and women across the Vietnamese diaspora to take on what feminist geographers Doreen Massey and Pat Jess (1995) call "a place in the world" in the age of globalization by the very enactment of various forms of capital across a specific transnational social field. The most striking example of this is the convertibility of low-worth capital (such as low income from the West) to high worth across social fields. In a transnational social field, as well, high-worth capital may be undermined in order to participate in international marriages. For example, highly educated women with high cultural capital in Saigon might undermine or deflect their cultural capital in a transnational social field because they view such capital as less meaningful when transferred overseas. A focus on various spatiotemporal locations reveals how participants in international marriages become what Sonita Sarker and Esha Niyogi De call "trans-status subjects," a term that "captures the fact that individuals, moving in the tracks created by global masculinist-capitalist power, are caught in transition from one (economic, social, political) status to another, at the same time as they try to redefine their places-turned-into-spaces" (2002, 8).

I have shown how and why the enactment of convertibility of various forms of capital creates transnational meanings through marriage by documenting the complex contours of everyday transnational life. This study underscores how gender is related to what Inderpal Grewal and Caren Kaplan (1994) call "scattered hegemonies," such as global economic structures, patriarchal nationalisms, "authentic" forms of tradition, and local structures of domination. In this way, I have done much of what Sherry Ortner calls "subaltern practice theory," in which we "look for the slippages in reproduction, the erosions of long-standing patterns, the moments of disorder and of outright resistance" (1996, 17).

The "aging" Vietnamese diaspora provides an acute example of contemporary international marriage migration for at least four reasons: because of the relatively recent patterns of Vietnamese out-migration over the past three decades; because Vietnam has only recently opened its door to the global economy; because of the imbalanced demographic patterns across the Vietnamese diaspora; and because of the position of overseas Vietnamese as relatively low-wage earners compared to other groups in the Asian diaspora. Much of what we know about historical and contemporary international marriages emphasizes unequal exchanges between the first and third worlds, thereby reducing international marriages to economic motivations. Indeed, in the course of doing this research, I found that the general phrase "international marriage" obscures important variations such as personal motives, social networks, material resources, legal rights of different nationals, and local and global economies, thereby producing dichotomous images of the "first" and "third" worlds, "traditional" and "modern," and of the "poor" and the "rich." The arguments outlined in this book complicate these dichotomies by providing an exploratory look at the cultural struggles and material realities that link immigrant men and the "global women" of the third world, augmenting research that examines the constitution of gender in migration streams (Goldring 2003; Grasmuck and Pessar 1991; Hondagneu-Sotelo 1994; Hondagneu-Sotelo 2003; Hondagneu-Sotelo and Avila 1997; Jones-Correa 1998a, 1998b; Smith 1998). International married people attempt to make meanings, envision possible futures, and create their place in the world by anchoring themselves in geographical as well as social spaces. They orient their transnational gaze on geographical spaces across a specific social field that allows them to remember the past or to make sense of possible futures. Such orientations are inscribed and constituted in multiple and intersecting social locations of gender, class, and ethnicity. Place making among diasporic subjects necessitates "construction, rather than merely a discovery, of difference" (Gupta and Ferguson 1997, 13), and frequently involves convertibility of power and powerlessness across social fields, which can be obstructed and enhanced simultaneously by lines of gender, class, and ethnicity, depending on which end of the transnational social field one observes.

Recent assessments (Hondagneu-Sotelo 2003; Mahler and Pessar 2006) recognize that we still have virtually no attention paid to the situation of men in the contemporary literature on gender and transmigration. In the scarce literature focusing on gender and transnational processes, scholars who have paid attention to the situation of men have highlighted issues orbiting around the "public lives" of transmigrants, for example, issues focusing on how men differ from women in forming and maintaining transnational ties with hometown associations because of their sense of displacement in countries of settlement. The concept of displacement and meanings of home are useful here, for as Wanni Anderson and Robert Lee remind us, "talking about diaspora and transnationalism without placing them in the broader context of displacement is to diminish the weight of exile, the notion of home, or conversely the act of recreating the new home place" (2005, 10). The research by Michael Jones-Correa (1998a, 1998b) and Robert C. Smith (1998), for instance, suggests two important gendered patterns among male transmigrants who forge relations with the homeland. First, immigrant men are more likely than immigrant women to shift their orientation to their home countries and to the prospect of return migration as they lose status in the United States. And second, immigrant women are more likely than immigrant men to interface with U.S. institutions. More recently, Luin Goldring has documented how the Mexican state's outreach programs reinforce gendered projects of transmigrants because they "offer a context for exercising substantive citizenship that enhances immigrant men's status and citizenship vis-à-vis the Mexican state while marginalizing women by excluding them from positions of power and status" (2003, 347). In all of these studies, it is mainly men at the lower rung of the U.S. labor market who are compelled to maintain strong ties with their homeland, an important finding to highlight because it specifies social locations in experiences of displacements among migrants. What emerges from these differences in how men and women across class backgrounds experience displacement and a need to maintain ties to the homeland is that, as Dorinne Kondo (1996) cautions, the notion of "home" may have different meanings depending on the social location of those in diaspora.

The focus on Vietnamese immigrant men who anchor themselves in the natal country as a response to labor-market marginality in the host country provides a different vantage point to consider in the research on gender and migration because it interrogates gender as a "constitutive" element of immigration by linking gender with other categories such as social class, migration history, colonial past, and a particular racialized experience (Hondagneu-Sotelo 2003, 9). I also see this work as a general contribution toward the field of masculinities. In the mid-1980s, a "new sociology of masculinity" (Carrigan, Connell, and Lee 1985) was proposed to in order to examine critically hegemonic power relations among men and between men and women. Since that framework was introduced, much of the scholarly work on the topic invokes the plural *masculinities* to account for the heterogeneity in the politics of masculinity. Yet, I suggest that we need more empirical studies on subaltern masculinities, especially among transnational and immigrant men. The narratives of the men in this study, for example, reveal how subaltern men construct their masculinity and sense of respectability given that their lives are placed "at the intersection and interstices of vast systems of power: patriarchy, racism, colonialism, and capitalism, to name a few" (Chen 1999, 589).

The Future of Vietnamese
International Marriages

Vietnamese diasporic subjects attempt to make their place in the world, and they believe that they have taken the right step to achieve that by going global. Place making requires extensive and complex converting of different forms of social, economic, cultural, and symbolic capital, and marriage is a key institution in processes of convertibility across transnational social fields. Place making in the diasporic context allows men and women to enact what anthropologist Henrietta Moore calls "fantasies of identity," which are "ideas about the kind of person one would like to be and the sort of person one would like to be seen to be by others" (1994, 66). These fantasies are anchored in a specific moment of marriage and migration as international couples wait to unite with each other. An obvious sequel to this project is to ask what happens once international Vietnamese couples physically unite. I anticipate to follow up on these couples in the near future.

Based on the fieldwork I have conducted, there are several possibilities for the future of Vietnamese international couples as the women migrate to join their husbands overseas. In a happy global story, men will join in the quiet feminist movement in Vietnam and leave behind the tradition they never had as they move forward with their new marriages so that, for example, women will, as Thoa from chapter 5 would, earn their own wage and spend it as they wish. I believe some, but few, men will join women in these changes. In a tragic global story, other couples may end in divorce, or worse, women will be abused by their husbands. I do not believe the latter will likely be the case. Many women thought about this possibility and had told me that their connection to transnational networks will ensure that they avoid abusive marriages. Of the women in my study, 75 percent, including virtually all the middle-class and college-educated women, have at least one overseas relative.

There has been extensive media attention to women in abusive coercive arranged marriages where dowries are often the reason for the coercion (Jana 2000; Molly Moore 1994; Narayan 1995; WIN News 1995), but virtually none of the women in my study were forced into arranged marriages, and certainly none of the middle-class and highly educated women. As Sunaina Marr Maira argues, the trope of arranged marriages "fits too neatly with Orientalized understanding of Asian cultures that sacrifice personal freedom to inexplicable but ancient traditions and collectivist control, unlike the individualist liberty of the rational, enlightened West" (2002, 153). This is the sort of trope that Lisa Lowe refers to as a master narrative that frequently "essentializes Asian American culture, obscuring the particularities and incommensurabilities of class, gender, and national diversities among Asians" (1996, 63). Historically, there has been no dowry system in marriage, arranged or otherwise, in Vietnam and, in fact, there are current legal sanctions against arranged marriages (Wisensale 1999). In Vietnam, the divorce rate has historically been low, although one researcher argues that divorce will probably rise with recent intensified modernizing processes (Tran 1995). What we do know is that arranged marriages tend to have low divorce rates, although there is now evidence that points to an increase in divorce where arrangements are made (Liao and Heaton 1992).

Once the women unite with their husbands through migration, I anticipate that virtually all of them will proceed with their marital life according to the politics of kinship, familial piety, and obligations regardless of their geographical identity or class status. The most likely future for these transpacific married couples will be situations in which men get what they want in the market of respect and women consent to a traditional family in the name of family and kinship. It is at this most fundamental level that this book considers how and why transnational mobilities can simultaneously challenge as well as reinforce patriarchy. "Instead of being a social equalizer that empowers all migrants alike," as Luis Guarnizo argues, "transnational migration tends to reproduce and even exacerbate class, gender, and regional inequalities" (1997, 281). Women will enjoy some aspects of modernity they can not acquire in Vietnam, but they will be burdened by tradition left behind there. Women like Trang, Thu, Thoa, and Thanh will enjoy an opportunity to participate in wage work when they migrate overseas, but they will be under familial surveillance across transnational social fields. In some ways, they will go from a patriarchal frying pan to a patriarchal fire, but with one big difference. In the West, their desire for gender equity will find more support, in a culture where women dare to leave their husbands if they are not treated equally. But the women in my study, whether they were self-identified "traditional" women like My-Xuan Quoc or "modern" women like Trang Le, Thu Vo, Thoa Dang, or Thanh Nguyen, have the burden of tradition in Vietnam to hold them back from choosing this option. For the politics of kinship, as Minh, Thanh's husband, pointed out, serves as the backdrop for why women like Thanh "must have a happy marriage." In a culture where divorce is stigmatized and where saving face is a sacred activity, if these transpacific wives daringly divorce their husbands, they will cause their family and kin a loss of reputation in Vietnam and overseas. If they stay in the marriage, they will give up their need for the respect, equality, and self-worth they think are waiting for them in overseas communities.

Many of the men in this study had the access and support of kin-based networks that initiated and carried through marriage arrangements for them. More important, they have strong traditions left behind in Vietnam to protect them against the instability of marriage. Before the end of this global story, and as the women wait to unite with their husbands, it seems the only thing Vietnamese transpacific wives have to look forward to is more waiting, waiting for men like their husbands, who live in modern countries, to simply respect women. For Vietnamese politics of kinship across the diaspora promise that transpacific couples regardless of their class makeup, marriageability, or understanding of gender, will remain married—for better or for worse.

Appendix A
Reflections on Methodology

Like many personal biographies that inform sociologists' work (Glassner and Hertz 2003), my fieldwork and interviews were shaped by my various sets of identity across the globe. In a classic article on the nature of the insider versus outsider role in social science research, Robert Merton wrote that "since we all occupy various statuses and have group affiliations of varying significance to us . . . differing situations activate different statuses which then and there dominate over the rival claims of other statuses" (1972, 25). My social position as an overseas Vietnamese refugee man who slowly crossed class lines profoundly shaped my status in different contexts while doing fieldwork across the Vietnamese diaspora. Throughout the project, I wondered about the impact of my shared ethnicity, my gender, and my social class in relations to the people I interviewed. My assumption from the beginning was that it would be easy for me to gain access to and interview people across the Vietnamese diaspora because of my shared ethnicity. But I quickly learned that my social location turned out to be much more complicated than I had expected, which is why I also believe that the dichotomized view of the researcher as either insider or outsider is problematic; my position across transnational social fields involved "shifting identifications amid a field of interpenetrating communities and power relations" (Narayan 1993, 671).

Before elaborating on the issue of gaining entry and offering some reflections on interviewing, I would like to speak about the complicated procedures involved in the fieldwork I conducted, to focus on how I got to know these couples initially, what the waiting period entailed, and the limitations of what I can capture about this "snapshot" of marriage and migration. It is important to remind the reader that the couples I got to know were transnationally separated after being married, as the men returned to their overseas locations and the women waited in Vietnam to unite with their husbands through migration. Thus, with few exceptions, transpacific couples faced a "migration waiting period" before wives could join their husbands abroad. The project was divided into a "bride phase" in Vietnam and a "groom phase" in the United States. Of all the interviews I conducted, 80 percent, including all of the initial ones, were done face-to-face; 12 percent (n = 22/181) were conducted in English, the rest in Vietnamese; 60 percent of the interviews lasted from two to five hours. I also conducted some recorded phone interviews that usually lasted about thirty minutes. Although I had research assistance throughout the entire project, all data collection, either through interviews or participant observation, was done by me or in my presence. I transcribed and translated about half of the interviews, and the rest were done by three research assistants in the United States. I listened to every interview to verify its accuracy in both transcriptions and translations. I coded and analyzed all of the data.

THE BRIDE PHASE IN VIETNAM

I sought names of couples from urban Saigon as well as rural Se Long in order to compare the marital experiences of brides who came from rural and urban areas. The residences of brides spanned all of the twelve districts in Saigon and two of the six districts in Se Long. For practical reasons, I limited the sample in Se Long to six neighboring villages located in two districts in order to cover a feasible geographical space. Since the original lists contained no telephone numbers and only addresses of transpacific wives in Vietnam and transpacific husbands in the diaspora, one of my research assistants in Vietnam drafted and sent letters to all the wives' homes, alerting them to my study and inviting them to participate. The letter informed the wives that I would visit their homes within the next few weeks. To obtain a probability sample of marriages, I picked every fourth name from the top to the bottom of the original two lists of names of couples in registered marriages that I received from the Department of Justice in Vietnam and went to the wives' houses in Saigon and in Se Long with no notice except for the letters my research assistant initially sent them. In Vietnamese culture, there is little social protocol for "calling ahead" or making appointments prior to visiting people's homes. Thus, I did not go beyond local social etiquette when I appeared at people's homes with little notice. In most cases, although not all, the married women were living with their natal family while waiting to migrate abroad to join their husbands. In these cases, I invited the transpacific wives as well as their family members to take part in the study because I was well aware that kin networks had a tremendous impact on decisions about marriage in Vietnam. In over 70 percent of the cases, I interviewed people several times over, although I only tape-recorded first and second interviews. Two transpacific wives in Saigon and nine in Se Long declined my invitation to participate in the study, giving a response rate of 86 percent (n = 69/80) for the bride phase of research.

THE GROOM PHASE IN THE UNITED STATES

After I chronicled the experiences of the wives in Vietnam, I turned to the husbands' side of the story—the men who married the women I met in Vietnam. At this point, none of the women had migrated to join their husbands in the United States. At first, when I returned to the United States in August 2000 from the bride phase of research in Vietnam, I intended to conduct telephone interviews with men located in the Vietnamese diaspora. The grooms in my sample who married the brides I met in Vietnam came from eight countries and sixteen U.S. states. Since going to all eight countries and sixteen states was not a practical decision for a project of this scope, I initially decided to interview the grooms over the phone, despite the limitations of using this method. I crafted and sent letters to all the grooms across the globe and invited them to participate in my study. The letter to the grooms informed them that I had met their wives in Vietnam, and fully described the nature of the study. By this time, most of the brides in Vietnam had already told their husbands about my project. Most, though not all, of the wives I met gave me the telephone numbers of their husbands. For those men whose telephone numbers I did not have, I attached a postcard asking them to reply with their telephone numbers. Unfortunately, when I called them, many of the grooms declined my invitation to participate in the study. Some never returned my calls, and some simply said they were too busy to talk on the phone. Some never returned the postcards I attached in the letter.

The high turn-down rate from transpacific husbands resembled a pattern also noted by other researchers who study men's perspectives on marriage and the family (Rubin 1976, 1994). In general, men are less likely than women to share information about family life. Furthermore, people are generally more reluctant to talk to researchers on the telephone than to talk in person. A large portion of the husbands who declined my telephone interviews, however, told me that if I came in person, they would grant an interview, or at least they did not rule it out when I broached this possibility. I suspected and confirmed that most of them were shy but also simultaneously curious about the study. Some of them just simply did not want to spend the little time they had to talk to me, given that many of them worked long hours.

I stopped pursuing phone interviews when I secured a grant that allowed me to go to four major metropolitan areas in the United States to meet some of the husbands. Over a three-month period from January through April 2001, I flew first to Los Angeles, then Seattle and Boston, and ended back in San Francisco, where I was based at the time. My chief purpose during this phase of research was to get to know twenty-three of the grooms who were located in those cities. Eleven of them were in the metropolitan area of Los Angeles, five in the San Francisco Bay area (including San Jose), four in Boston, and three in Seattle. I spent six weeks in Los Angeles, two weeks each in Seattle and Boston, and remaining and final segment of work in the San Francisco Bay area, where I was living at the time. Given that they had already received letters and phone calls from my assistants and me, I approached the husbands in the same way as I did the wives—by appearing at their homes, introducing myself, and asking them to participate in the study. I even approached those who had rejected a telephone interview if they were located in or around one of the four metropolitan areas I visited.

Unlike transpacific wives, transpacific husbands were recruited through a nonprobability sample in and around four metropolitan areas. One of the limitations of this project lies in the fact I was not able to obtain the perspectives and experiences of all the grooms who married the brides I met in Vietnam. In the end, I got to know about 40 percent (n = 28/69) of all the husbands in the study. These grooms included five I met in Vietnam during the bride phase of research while they were visiting their wives: two from Australia, and one each from Paris, Toronto, and Kansas. This meant that in total, I got to know twenty-four U.S.-based husbands (twenty-three during the U.S.

segment of my research, and one man from Kansas whom I met among the five men visiting Vietnam) and four husbands living in other parts of the diaspora. Altogether, U.S. men in my sample constituted a little over 50 percent (n = 24/47) of all the husbands from the United States who married the women I interviewed in Vietnam. In total, then, the U.S.-based husbands I got to know and interviewed constituted one-third (n = 24/69) of all the men who married the women I met in Vietnam. The United States was a good choice for the groom phase of the project not only because of limited resources but also because the United States is the country of residence of over 55 percent of all Viet Kieu (Long 2004). Vietnamese American men constituted about 68 percent (n = 47) of all the grooms in my study.

GAINING ENTRY

The issue of gaining entry in Vietnam and in the United States is peculiar because of the nature of the subject and the way I got to know informants. If I had used snowball sampling, gaining entry would certainly have been much easier than getting to know informants through marriage registration lists. Snowball sampling would also have been a good choice because by the time that I decided to officially start working on this topic, I had many ties to Vietnam, ties that would have informally gotten me names of couples on the transpacific marriage market. As I developed stronger interests in the topic, I got to know at least a dozen overseas men in the United States who had returned to Vietnam for wives. I also knew many travel agents, including some close friends and family members, who provided services to help transpacific couples process paperwork for the wives to migrate and join their husbands abroad. Some of these agencies were willing to introduce me to transpacific couples. In addition, many of my father's kinfolk—the relatives "left behind" when we migrated—were also living in the Mekong Delta, from where we originated. Some of them knew women on the transpacific marriage market. Despite these connections and the potential advantages in using snowball sampling, I concluded that by using the lists of names of registered married people provided by the Vietnamese Department of Justice, I had at least two very important advantages. First, it swiftly gave me a large number of respondents. Second, it forced me to learn about the process of international marriage sponsorship because I had to trace the steps involved in marriage registrations, and learned that there was the "migration waiting period" in these people's lives, a period that is crucial to consider in my analysis of these marriages.

Initially, I suspected that officials at the Institute were trying to divert my plans to use snowball sampling in hopes that I would provide "gifts" to them so they would proceed with helping me obtain government permissions to conduct research. But later on, as I got to know them in the various phases of my research project, I concluded that there was no reason to believe that officials at the Institute were so motivated, since no one ever asked for gifts and I never offered anything. It was clear that officials at the Institute simply intellectually favored random sampling. Most of the people there were trained in quantitative sociology in various parts of the world. They were not acquainted with methods of qualitative sociology, where snowballing is a common sampling procedure. At one point, one of the researchers at the Institute told me that he had never heard of people doing sociological work using snowball sampling, and that I simply did not know what I was doing. This, of course, reflects the hegemony of quantitative methods in the social sciences generally.

Despite the advantages in sampling by selecting names from marriage registration lists, gaining entry to people's lives can be awkward with this sampling method. My only strategy was to write to the people I wanted to interview, and then to visit their homes. In Vietnam, I thought about having my research assistant visit the brides' homes first, then report to me about the feasibility of visiting them myself. At the time, I could not afford to use this strategy in the United States with such a large sample because it would have been too costly. But in Vietnam I was able to convert my own wages to hire assistants much more cheaply than I would have been able to in the United States.

When I started to visit people's homes, I was nervous at first, not because I am a shy person. After all, I decided early in my career that I find qualitative work much more interesting because I like to get to know people's inner worlds, and that requires, I believe, a certain kind of personality. I was also not, as a man, particularly shy about studying the lives of women. For me, it is a situation similar to that when people study across racial groups, which is what many sociologists do. It is a matter of reference points and crossing lines of difference. Surprisingly, my initial nervousness was not about myself, but I was afraid that the wives I would visit would decline to participate in the study because of Sang from the Institute, who was required to accompany me to all my first interviews as part of my agreement to obtain permission for doing this project. First, he was much darker than I am, which clearly indicated that we came from different social worlds. I was afraid that people might find it odd that two very different men (one clearly from overseas, and one local) were visiting their homes and wanting to understand their private lives. Second, Sang was from northern Vietnam, so his accent was different from mine. I was afraid that potential respondents would think of Sang as an immigration official because of his northern accent, since many officials are originally from the north. Coming from a family of premigrants and emigrants, I knew that locals were always afraid of immigration officials for a wide variety of reasons.

I soon learned that Sang was an impediment to the research process when I introduced us as a pair: Sang as an "official" from the Institute for Social Sciences and I as a researcher from the United States. It made the whole thing too official, which I believe turned people off. Yet, ironically, precisely because potential respondents thought that we were officials, they did not decline our requests for interviews. The problem was that when people gave us interviews, they were bad ones, most often with very simple answers. For example, on one of the first interviews I did in Saigon, our transcript was the following:

HUNG THAI: Can you begin by telling me what you do daily?
RESPONDENT: I work.
HUNG THAI: What kind of work do you do?
RESPONDENT: Work for money.
HUNG THAI: Where do you work?
RESPONDENT: In Saigon.
HUNG THAI: Can you tell me more about the kind of work you do daily?
RESPONDENT: I type and make phone calls, and some other stuff.

This brief excerpt from one transcript early on in my research shows that there were obvious improvements to be made. After the fourth bad interview, Sang and I decided I could introduce him as my research assistant, rather than as an official from the Institute. I knew that the Vietnamese easily accept social hierarchies. Once I began to introduce Sang as my assistant, which eventually became the reality of his role in working with me, the interviews improved dramatically. The respondents were much more willing to accept the social hierarchy of us as a pair than to see Sang as an official and me as a researcher from overseas.

Despite the difficulties in Vietnam, I found that gaining entry with grooms and their families in the United States much more difficult. In Vietnam, I had more time to get to know brides and their families. I knew that if the first interview did not go well, I could come back for a second, third, and even fourth interview. I also knew that subsequent interviews could be spaced out over weeks or even months because I was in Vietnam for eight months of intensive fieldwork. For the grooms in the United States, I had to make the best use of my limited time, since I was in each city for less than a month. On the other hand, I was not faced with other tasks, like getting permission and paperwork, which I had faced in Vietnam. By the time I started to do interviews in the United States, I was also well versed in the culture of Vietnamese international marriages and I knew fairly well what I wanted to ask the grooms.

The main reason why it was more difficult in the United States, I believe, was because American culture generally requires people to call ahead before they stop by someone's home. Although most of the men in my study were immigrants and were more "Vietnamese" than they were "American," I followed American norms since I got to know them in the United States. My own upbringing in an immigrant family in the United States taught me that even though we were Vietnamese, we always called people ahead of time prior to making visits to people's homes. This limited the number of times I could visit grooms, because I had to make appointments for interviews, whereas for the brides, I never had to make appointments.

By the time I got to the groom's sites, I knew fairly well the situations of their lives, and had good expectations of what I wanted to ask them. Yet I sometimes had difficulty in establishing rapport. In contrast, in Vietnam, I never felt awkward just stopping by people's homes whether or not I knew them. By the time I got to the groom's locations, I had already written them letters and for most of them, I also had their telephone numbers. And most knew that I was coming. But there were five men who did not provide phone numbers, so I assumed that they knew I was coming only through the letters I sent them prior to my arrival. Generally, for the grooms that I was able to call in advance, I came at their convenience, and for those I was not able to call, I stopped by at various times of the day because I knew that most of them did not have regular work schedules.

The most awkward encounter I had was in the suburb of Orange County with a groom who I did not have phone contact with prior to stopping by. When I arrived one late afternoon, the groom was surprised when he opened the door, as I would have been, too, because he did know when I was coming. In the letter I sent the grooms, I gave them a two-week window within which I would visit their homes. When the thirty-two-year-old man opened the door, he was completely quiet. I initiated a greeting in Vietnamese, "Hi, how are you. My name is Hung Thai." He gave no reply. I knew that I always had to have a little introduction prepared for shy people. In this case, I proceeded by telling him how I met his wife in Vietnam by referring to her name and I also told him how she told me that she missed him terribly given their distance. Then, I reminded him that I wrote him a letter not too long ago. After about five minutes of my introduction, he motioned his hand for me to shake, but still in silence. Then, he gestured his hand for me to enter his house, where I went to sit in a chair across from his mother who was living with him. I was relieved to see another person, but felt intrusive and unwelcome since the groom was so indifferent about my visit. It was at this moment that I realized I had to really use my Vietnamese colloquial language, undermine the formal language of research, and also establish rapport with the family of the grooms as I did with the families of the brides in Vietnam. When this man motioned me into his house, he ran upstairs, leaving me alone with his mother.

Of course, I felt very odd that he just ran upstairs leaving me alone with his mother when we had not even been introduced. I took this opportunity to introduce myself to the woman sitting on the sofa. And then I continued by asking if she had been back to Vietnam. We continued making references to common places in Vietnam that we had visited. While talking to this woman, I realized that about ten minutes had passed and the man I came to interview was still upstairs. I was getting nervous that he did not want to see me at all and was hoping that I would leave in his absence, and I was also nervous that I would run out of things to say to his mother. To my surprise, he came down fifteen minutes later with a stack of papers. As it turned out, he was gathering the paperwork upstairs that he had started to sponsor his wife in Vietnam. He was having difficulty with the trails of paperwork, and he asked me if I knew the information well. I took that opportunity to tell him all I knew, which was a lot by this point, about the process of sponsorship. We proceeded with going through his paperwork, and I stayed for well over five hours to talk to him and his mother.

Rapport

With each informant I interviewed in Vietnam and in the United States, I worked hard to hide certain statuses while at the same time foregrounding others in order to develop rapport. Laura Nadar suggests that rapport "may have nothing to do with being reasonable or pleasant in the field, or liking and admiring the people with whom one works. . . . [It] refers to the ability to cope with a field situation in such a way that work is possible" (1986, 113). I found it much easier to develop rapport with the women I interviewed than with their husbands. In Vietnam, rapport was easily achieved with the women because of their curiosity about life abroad; my own experience as an immigrant, which they were curious about but had not yet experienced; and our similar class positionings. The women were almost always interested in learning about a combination of my unusual career choice as a Vietnamese American man, my life in the United States, and my family's history in Vietnam.

For the same reason that this class positioning helped to establish rapport with the women, it impeded my rapport with some of the husbands. Generally, I received two kinds of treatments from the husbands. They found my choice of profession either admirable, or they found it very foreign and were uninterested. Both situations created problems. In the first scenario, they often gave me too much deference, which did not make the interviews go well, and in these circumstances I tried to emphasize my working-class roots. In the latter situation, they did not care about my aspiration and so they did not want to give me their time. In both situations, I tried to gauge early on how they perceived me. I would disclose my class identity accordingly. I also had to decide early on how much information about myself I would disclose to the men and women in the study. My first inclination always was to reciprocate information. Just as I expected them to share with me their thoughts and emotions, I felt obligated to reciprocate because they, too, were interested in me. I do not know if this was the right decision to make, but I do think that sharing information with respondents increased my rapport with them. I believe that my respondents were almost always able to tell if I was genuine when talking to them about my private life.

One thing I learned quickly in Vietnam was that in order to develop rapport with the women I had to pick up the habit of smoking, something I did not do until I started this project. Smoking is a sign of masculinity and maturity in Vietnam, so that in order to be taken seriously, a man must participate in it. Smoking became an important practice in the interview process in Vietnam, much more so than in the United States. This was because many of the grooms did not smoke when I met them in the United States, but in Vietnam, I knew few men who did not. At every interview in Vietnam, Sang and I were offered cigarettes. I realized sooner, rather than later, that when Sang or I did not smoke, women were much less willing to talk to us.

We seemed too official if we were not casual "Vietnamese men," who smoked profusely.

Another strategy of developing rapport in Vietnam was to have my mother come with me during interviews. She became an enormous asset during my second interviews with brides and their families. For example, on many occasions, my mother started conversations that, at the beginning, I had a harder time initiating. On one of the first occasions, for instance, when I tried to understand the issue of money in these international relationships, we visited a bride's family on a day when the bride received a remittance from her husband in California. I initially felt uncomfortable, because of my own "American" etiquette, about asking my respondents how much money they were receiving in remittances from their overseas kin. My mother, however, had no hesitations about asking questions involving money, or for that matter, whatever she wanted to know. On this occasion, she just asked in a matter-of-fact way, "How much did you get today?" The bride replied, "only $200." Nothing else was said about that money, and we continued on with other topics. I learned through my mother that while formal rituals and ceremonial activities are part of everyday life, the Vietnamese are generally frank and straightforward. Issues of money (how much one makes, how much one has), weight, education, and martial status are all askable. By the time that I finished my fieldwork in Vietnam, there were few issues I was unable to ask directly upon meeting a stranger for the first time.

I found that in some situations, it was effective, if not necessary, to highlight the fact that my job was in academia. For instance, when I met Minh, the assistant cook from Washington about whom I write in chapter 6, he was initially diplomatic at best, and generally indifferent and uninterested. Our first interview, therefore, was mediocre. But at the end of this first interview, he asked me why I was collecting all the interviews, even though I had told him at the beginning of the interview that it was for a research project. I then explained to him that part of being a professor required doing research and writing books and articles, and that collecting interviews was a part of that process. All of sudden, he became overly friendly to me. Unfortunately, by that time, it was too late to continue the interview. That evening when I returned to the hotel where I was staying, he called me to see if I wanted to come over the following day to have dinner at the restaurant where he worked. At dinner the next day, he told me much more about his past than he did in the first interview, how he loved school, and how he just did not have the opportunity to continue with schooling once he migrated to the United States. He even went as far to tell me that he admired professors more than any other occupation. This incident with Minh illustrates how disclosing my aspirations, my career choice, and therefore, upward mobility sometimes helped to enhance rapport with respondents that otherwise would not have been possible if I had not disclosed the information.

There were other cases, however, where I had to emphasize my working-class past and downplay the privileges that come with being upwardly mobile. For example, when I interviewed a thirty-eight-year-old man who was a waiter at a Vietnamese restaurant in Los Angeles, he asked me about why I was interested in studying Vietnamese international marriages. I told him that I had stumbled upon the topic when I visited my mother in Vietnam. He then asked me how many times I had been to Vietnam. By this time, I knew that some of the men could not afford to return frequently, both prior to and after their married lives. I had to decide whether or not to tell this man that I had been back seven times in the span of three years. Most overseas Vietnamese I knew return every other year at most if they had close family members, and few people I interviewed made yearly visits. I decided that I would tell him the truth, because I wanted him to know that I was genuinely interested in the topic and that I had made great efforts in trying to learn about the process. I also prefaced the information by saying that my mother was in Vietnam and that I needed to see her often. By telling him about my mother, I had hoped that he would sympathize with my personal history. But I learned quickly that I had made a huge mistake. This man got angry at me, proceeding to tell me that I did not know anything about his life because we were very different people. "How could you understand anything about what I do?" he asked, implying that I could not understand what it was like to wait tables at a restaurant. I told him that because I did not know much, I was trying to understand. I also said that I come from poverty and grew up in the housing projects, and that my own father had toiled in many harsher jobs than waiting tables at a restaurant. He was not convinced that I shared his class identity because he started to make remarks about my "fancy" clothes, which were jeans and a T-shirt, and he became vulgar. I thought he would calm down and finish the interview after I gave him the opportunity to vent, but instead, he got up, and simply asked me to leave his house. I politely left with embarrassment, not sure what had really happened. I called him the next day, but he never returned my call.

Despite some difficult moments and some difficult interviewees, such as the one I just described, I found that for the most part, once they got to know me, most people enjoyed talking about themselves, learning about what I had to say, and what I planned to do with the interviews. Some people thought sociology also included social work and family therapy (which is true in Vietnam), and so many of them sought my advice about their marriages. The women frequently asked me what I thought their lives would be like overseas. Many of the brides and their families came to visit me frequently in Saigon. Some of the grooms in the San Francisco Bay area visited me and invited me to their homes for special events. Many in the

United States and in Vietnam continued to stay in touch once I finished collecting data.

But despite my general sense that I succeeded in doing interviews and fieldwork, there were certainly variations in the quality of interviews and variations in rapport and degree of comfort among my respondents. I did not let my level of rapport with individual respondents dictate the data. For instance, there were interviewees that I got to know better than the ones I use in the case studies for this book. But some of the people I got to know better had lives that did not necessarily illuminate what I felt were important dimensions of Vietnamese international marriages.

INTERVIEWS AS EVIDENCE

Although I did participant observations with eight families in Saigon and followed grooms in their locations in the United States, I see the evidence for this book as mostly data from interviews. I rely much more on what people said than what I observed for data analysis. This is not to say that the study does not have elements of an ethnography, because I studied the lives of people in specific places and social contexts that required me to see how they lived. The best data I got out of visits to people's homes were the mundane, the ordinary stuff of life that captured so much of what I write in this book—dusty tables, picture frames, gifts from overseas, the special shoes from an overseas relative, the worried face, the overly neat hair, photo albums, and so on. Some of the interviews were illuminating precisely because of the specific places that I conducted them. My approach to providing information on the everyday contours of interviewee's lives was only possible because I got to see the everyday. For instance, when I interviewed Trang in chapter 1, it did not occur to me until our latter interviews that she had received the white cordless telephone from her husband, Hieu. In Saigon, I knew many families with cordless telephones and since I knew Trang had gone to school in Saigon, my assumption at first was that she had bought it there before returning to her village. It was not until the third interview with Trang that I casually asked about it and I learned that Hieu had sent her the gift. Over the course of the next week, I interviewed Trang four more times to learn about the social history of that phone, which was sitting on the table between us each time we did our interviews. Indeed, this was the sort of ethnographic detail embedded in my interviews that frequently surfaced in the course of learning about the lives of individuals involved in the contemporary Vietnamese international marriage market.

APPENDIX B
CHARACTERISTICS OF THE SAMPLE

HERE I DISCUSS THE characteristics of the sample in this study, considering ethnic variations, place of residence at the time of marriage, educational attainment, occupational status, age, age differences, marital history, transnational networks, and current living arrangements. For the grooms, I also discuss modes of migration, year of migration, and citizenship status.

ETHNIC VARIATIONS

Although Vietnam has a long history of ethnic minorities, the majority of the respondents were ethnic Vietnamese, with over 90 percent (n = 62/69) of couples consisting of ethnic Vietnamese brides and grooms. Those who belonged to a minority ethic group were all of Chinese origin, this being the largest single ethnic minority in Vietnam. Currently, more than 1.5 million of Vietnam's approximately 80 million people are ethnic Chinese. Most of the ethnic Chinese live in the south and are concentrated in District Five's *Cho Lon* (Large Market) in Saigon. One journalist has observed that as many as 80 percent of the Chinese in Vietnam have overseas relatives (Hiebert 1996). Although there are other ethnic minorities in Vietnam, for example hill tribes in the central Highlands and Cambodians in the Mekong Delta, the only ethnic variation in this sample were Vietnamese immigrant men of Chinese origin who returned to Vietnam for wives.

Vietnamese men of Chinese origin who returned to marry Vietnamese women constituted 3 percent (n = 2); no Vietnamese man returned to marry a woman of Chinese origin. In the case of 6 percent of the couples (n = 4), both groom and bride were of Chinese origin. There was one mixed-race groom (who had a French father and a Vietnamese mother). I decided to include these few ethnic and racial variations in the sample even though they are not the subjects of the chapters I present in this book so as to demonstrate the varying contexts of Vietnamese out-migration, though I recognize the social and cultural distinctiveness of the Chinese Vietnamese and of mixed-race Vietnamese individuals worldwide.

PLACE OF RESIDENCE

Of the wives, 70 percent (n = 48/69) came from urban Saigon, and 30 percent (n = 21) came from one of six neighboring rural villages in two districts in the province of Se Long. About 95 percent of the grooms (n = 65) came from the four core countries of the United States, Canada, Australia, and France; 68 percent (n = 47) of the grooms came from the United States, 13 percent (n = 9) from Canada, 9 percent (n = 6) from Australia, and 4.5 percent (n = 3) from France. The rest included one each from England, Norway, Germany, and Belgium. The U.S.-based grooms were from sixteen states; about two-thirds of them lived and worked in four states: 40 percent were from California and 27 percent were from Texas, Washington, and Massachusetts. There were two each in the states of Mississippi, Kansas, New York, and New Jersey. Finally, there was one each in Louisiana, Georgia, Virginia, Oregon, Maryland, Colorado, Pennsylvania, and Arizona. Of the twenty-eight grooms I got to know, eleven were in Los Angeles, five were in the San Francisco Bay area, four were in Boston, and three were in Seattle. I met the remaining five grooms in Vietnam. Two of these were from Australia, and one each was from Paris, Toronto, and Kansas.

AGE AND MARITAL HISTORY

As figures A.1 and A.2 show, the distribution of brides' ages ranged from twenty to sixty-three, and grooms from twenty to sixty-nine. The average ages of transpacific wives and husbands were 30.5 and 36, respectively. I divided the ages of wives and husbands into four age brackets by decade, starting with the twenties. The modal age group for wives was 20–30, with forty-one of them in that age group, whereas the modal age group for husbands was 31–40, with thirty-one of them in that age group. Only two brides were fifty years old or older, whereas eight of the grooms were fifty or over. If I disregarded all grooms and brides who were fifty years of age and over, the sample would contain sixty-seven brides with an average age of 29.8 and sixty-one grooms with an average age of 33.5. I point this out to illustrate that grooms and brides fifty years and older were somewhat anomalous in the sample.

While 78 percent (n = 54) of the couples involved never-married people, 22 percent (n = 15) were couples in which at least one of the members was in a remarriage market. I refer to *remarriage individuals* as those for whom a transpacific marriage

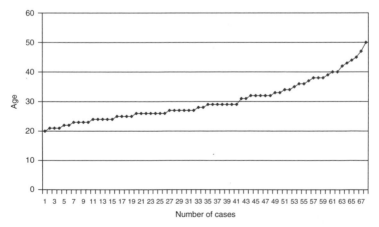

A-1. Age Distribution of Transpacific Brides in This Study

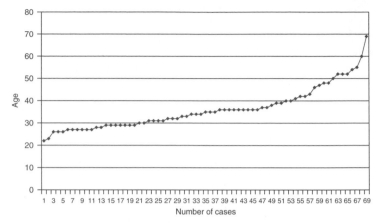

A-2. Age Distribution of Transpacific Grooms in This Study

was a remarriage regardless of whether or not their transpacific spouse was part of a remarriage. I refer to *remarriage couples* as couples in which both partners were in a remarriage. A total of 13 percent (n = 9) of the grooms were either married, divorced, or widowed prior to their international marriages, with six divorced, two widowed, and one separated from an extralegal marriage in the United States. Of the brides, 14 percent (n = 10) were divorced before their international marriages. None was a widow, and none was separated from a previous marriage—a telling gendered story about remarriages in Vietnamese culture. Of the fifteen couples in the remarriage market, five were cases in which both partners were in a remarriage market. Coincidentally, about 9 percent of the brides and 9 percent of the grooms had at least one child from a previous marriage, though these people did not necessarily marry each other.

Of all never-married individuals, the average age was 30 for brides and 33.5 for grooms. Of remarriage individuals, the average age was 37.5 for brides and 53 for grooms. Of all the couples in which both partners were never married (n = 54),

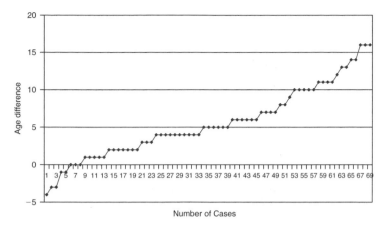

A-3. Distribution of Age Differences between Transpacific Grooms and Brides in This Study

the average age of the brides was 29 compared to 33.5 for grooms. Remarriage individuals and couples were generally older than never-married people. For the most part, individuals in international marriages were never-married people at the time of marriage and were generally older than most single adults in their local contexts, suggesting that they prolonged their single status.

DIFFERENCES IN AGE

The differences in age between grooms and brides were not unusual in this study, and it is not unusual for husbands to be substantially older than their wives in Vietnam (Nguyen 1997). Figure A.3 illustrates the distribution of differences in age between grooms and brides in this study. Differences ranged from −4 to 16. Five of the brides were older than grooms, an unusual occurrence in the Vietnamese marriage gradient, with the biggest difference being four years. Transpacific grooms were on average 5.5 years older than brides. There were three anomalous cases of grooms who were fifteen years older than brides, but 61 percent (n = 42) of the brides were five or fewer

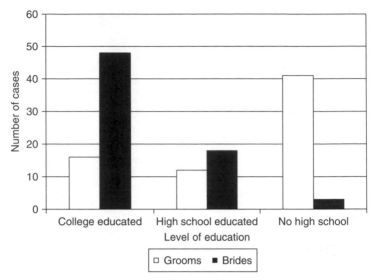

A-4. Educational Attainment of Grooms and Brides in This Study

years younger than grooms, and 81 percent (n = 52) of the brides were ten or fewer years younger than grooms. When I started this project, many Vietnamese across the diaspora told me that they knew many old men who returned for "young girls." I believe these cases do exist, but they were rare, and the rare ones were often sensationalized.

EDUCATIONAL ATTAINMENT
AND OCCUPATIONAL STATUS

Figure A.4 illustrates that 70 percent (n = 48) of the brides in my study had at least a college education, and of these women, 40 percent (n = 19/48) had an advanced degree. Compared to the brides, only 23 percent (n = 16/69) of the grooms had a college degree, of which one (less than 1.5 percent) had an advanced degree. Of grooms who held a college degree, over half (n = 9/16) earned the degree in Vietnam before they migrated to the United States, which generally did not help them in Western labor markets. In other words, of all the grooms, only 11.5 percent (n = 8/69) earned a college education after migration. In contrast to the wives, about 60 percent (n = 41/69) of the husbands had no high school education, while three of the wives had no high school education. Twelve grooms and eighteen brides had high school degrees, but no college education.

One of the most difficult tasks of this project is to compare the status of men and women relative to their local contexts, given the extremely unequal global situations in which they were embedded. Although there are many limitations to my comparisons of social class, I talk about the social class of wives mainly by referring to their educational levels and the social class of grooms mainly by referring to their incomes. This is because the men and women in this study generally marked their social status in those ways. Thus, social class is no doubt a gendered experience. In general, there are many discrepancies in immigrants' experiences of class and educational levels and in their ability to "translate" schooling to the kinds of work they do. The most profound example is the situation of highly educated women from the Philippines who go all over the world to do domestic work (Parrenas 2001b).

I found that, in general, grooms talked and made meanings of self by referring first to their income as a status marker, before they talked about their educational attainment; this was particularly true for low-wage workers, who generally dodged the question of educational attainment. Wives, on the other hand, talked extensively about their education as a status marker and in self-making, in part, because they often used Viet Kieu as a reference point, and it would have been virtually impossible for most of the women to assert status if they compared their third-world income with incomes in the first world. Still, even though I discuss social class based on wives' education and husbands' incomes, I divided the occupations and professions of grooms and brides into three main levels relative to their local contexts: high-wage, medium-wage, and low-wage. These generally translated respectively to "highly skilled," "semi-skilled," and "low-skilled" work, although I am aware of the problems in linking skills with wages. Many popularly known "low-skilled" jobs that pay little money require an enormous amount of skill, a point that has been articulated by Barbara Ehrenreich (2001) in her discussion of domestic work.

Those who generally earned the minimum legal or socially acceptable wage for their local contexts were classified as low-wage workers, although I understand that employers can easily dodge legal sanctions as they employ immigrants. For the Vietnamese in 2000 dollars, low-wage work generally paid anywhere from VND 500,000 to 800,000 per month (US$33–$53). For Americans, this meant about $6 to $8 per hour. I also researched wage differentials in other diasporic contexts and did the appropriate comparisons to classify the various kinds of jobs men did in their local contexts. Except in a few cases, the men who did low-wage work were also less educated than their wives; most of these grooms barely had a grade school education. However, I do not wish simply to link low-wage work with less education, and vice versa, though education and income are generally linked. I understand, for example, that plumbers may earn more money than teachers.

In the low-wage category, income was usually earned by the hour, with little job stability. Among medium-wage workers, there was more flexibility, and their jobs generally earned a salary but with few benefits (such as vacation time). In Vietnam, medium-wage usually meant VND 1 to 1.5 million (US$66–$100). In the United States, depending on the location, this usually meant somewhere in the mid-$20,000s, but below $40,000. These jobs generally involved some kind of trade such as tailoring or electric repair. High-wage workers in Vietnam generally earned at least VND 2 million (US$133), though many earned well above that amount. In contrast, for U.S. earners in the Vietnamese American contexts, high-wage jobs usually started at $40,000.

All grooms worked for a wage, whereas 78 percent of brides (n = 54) did so. The vast majority of grooms (81 percent) worked in low-wage jobs that were usually unskilled work such as dishwashing, janitorial/custodial, assembly line production, and truck driving. About 10 percent (n = 7) worked in jobs that required high-skilled labor. All of these were engineers except for one social worker in England with a master's degree. The remaining 9 percent (n = 6) were in medium-wage jobs such as reception work at a large hotel, carpentry, jewelry making, tailoring, and so on. In contrast to the grooms, wage-earning brides were predominately concentrated in high-wage jobs.

Of the fifty-four brides who worked, 57 percent (n = 31) were in high-wage jobs that usually required a college education. For example, there were two physicians, one lawyer, over a dozen teachers (most of whom were highly regarded in their circles either as English teachers or as teachers trained in the city who had returned to their villages), and seven who worked as translators for foreign companies such as IBM and Citibank. About 39 percent (n = 21) were in semiskilled work such as tailoring, secretarial work, and cooking; the remaining 4 percent (n = 2) were in low-wage jobs, one factory assembly-line worker and one street-food vendor. A surprising finding was that approximately three-fourths of the brides lived in families with hired domestic help, regardless of their work, so that for example, teachers who made US$80 a month in the Mekong Delta could pay someone US$20 per month to be a full-time servant. I note this to convey the magnitude of differences in standards of living one could achieve in the Mekong Delta, which might help us understand the enormous power of convertibility of capital across social fields.

TABLE B-1

Marriage Pairings Based on Women's Level of Education and Men's Income in This Study

Number of Cases	Brides' Level of Education	Grooms' Wages
2	No high school	Low-wage men
16	High school	Low-wage men
38	College-educated	Low-wage men
0	No high school	Medium-wage men
0	High school	Medium-wage men
6	College-educated	Medium-wage men
1	No high school	High-skilled men
2	High school	High-skilled men
4	College-educated	High-skilled men

Table B.1 shows the pairings of marriages based on women's education and men's level of income. One unique case was the situation of a high-wage man who married a non-wage-earning woman who had no high school education, the only couple in my study involving a high-wage man and a woman with no high school degree (either employed or not). They are the subject of chapter 7. An unexpected scenario was the statistically dominant type of couples, which I address in chapter 6, involving college-educated women in Vietnam married to overseas Vietnamese men who did low-wage work. These couples constituted 55 percent (n = 38) of the couples in my study.

TRANSNATIONAL NETWORKS

For purposes of describing transnational networks of grooms and brides, I divide their family members into four different types of networks: 1) parents, 2) siblings, 3) uncles, aunts, or grandparents, 4) and all other relatives (such as cousins). I chose these categories in order not simply to bifurcate Vietnamese families into immediate (siblings, children, parents) and non-immediate relatives (all other), thereby maintaining some of the distinctions embedded in complex Vietnamese rules of kinship (Luong 1990). Most brides had family ties abroad and all grooms had family ties in Vietnam. Over half of all grooms and brides were part of transnational families in which core family members (parents, siblings, aunt and uncle, and grandparent) were dispersed in at least three countries. Almost 75 percent (n = 51) of the brides had a parent, sibling, aunt/uncle, or grandparent living overseas. Many had complex networks of relations living abroad. Among the college-educated women, all except two (n = 45/47), had transnational networks overseas. Of all the brides, 38 percent (n = 26/69) had families and kin in the overseas community where their husbands resided; 12 percent (n = 8/69) had at least one parent abroad; and 25 percent (n = 17/69) had at least one sibling abroad.

Overall, if one examines social networks of international migrants, there are far more people in any social network who stay put than those who migrate. For this reason, it is easier to identify and calculate how many and which relatives brides had abroad than to do so for grooms. Grooms' transnational networks were more complex because, on average, they had more kin members in Vietnam than brides had in the diaspora. In contrast to the brides, all the grooms had at least one relative in Vietnam, which meant that no groom, probably like all Vietnamese emigrants of the past three decades, left Vietnam with their entire kin network. The grooms' networks in Vietnam were also more "immediate" than the networks of the brides in overseas Vietnamese communities; 29 percent (n = 20/69) of the grooms had at least one parent in Vietnam and 23 percent (n = 16/69) had at least one sibling in Vietnam.

Current Living Arrangements

Most brides lived with their parents before they married and continued to do so while waiting to migrate overseas. Some of

the brides and grooms reorganized household arrangements
after they married, particularly if grooms had parents and other
immediate families in Vietnam. Some brides, for example, went
to live with their husbands' families after marriage, some on a
"part-time" basis. Of all the grooms, 41 percent (n = 28/69)
lived by themselves in their overseas communities, 32 percent
(n = 22) lived with at least one of their parents, 12 percent
(n = 8) with other relatives, and 16 percent (n = 11) shared
housing with a nonrelative.

MODE OF MIGRATION

Almost all of the grooms (96 percent, n = 66/69) gained entry
into the Vietnamese diaspora in one of five ways: 1) as refugees
who were evacuated from Saigon by the U.S. government during the few days immediately before the fall of Saigon on April
30, 1975; 2) as "boat refugees" from the mid 1970s until the early
1990s; 3) as family reunification migrants in the U.S. Orderly
Departure Program (ODP); 4) as family reunification migrants
stipulated by current contemporary migration policies in their
respective countries; 5) or as part of the Humanitarian
Organization Program of 1989 (H.O.), an official agreement
between the United States and the Socialist Republic of
Vietnam that allowed Vietnamese political prisoners, current
and former detainees in reeducation camps, to migrate to the
United States. The remaining three men consisted of one born
in the United States, one who migrated with his half sibling
through the Amerasia Program of 1988, and a third who
migrated with his mother to France as a child (his mother married a Frenchman in the 1950s).

Of the men who left in the usual ways, 7 percent
(n = 5/66) migrated through the airlift efforts of the American
government several days immediately before the fall of Saigon
on April 30, 1975; 53 percent (n = 35/66) were boat refugees,
18 percent (n = 12/66) came through ODP, 9 percent

(n = 6/66) came as H.O.s (as they are referred to in overseas Vietnamese communities), and 12 percent (n = 8/66) migrated through contemporary family-reunification programs in their respective countries. Regardless of the mode of migration, 40 percent (n = 27/66) of the grooms were independent migrants, that is, men who migrated by themselves either as adults or as children. Many grooms intended to sponsor their parents and families abroad. However, only six of these grooms, all of whom were boat refugees, had been able to sponsor their parents after they resettled.

GROOMS' YEAR OF MIGRATION AND CITIZENSHIP STATUS

Grooms varied widely in the year of their migration. Of all sixty-nine, only one was born overseas (in the United States), and one migrated before 1975. This latter man migrated to France in 1955 as a toddler. So although sixty-seven of the grooms migrated after 1975, sixty-eight of them were born in Vietnam. For the sixty-eight grooms born in Vietnam who later migrated to the West, figure A.5 shows the distribution of their

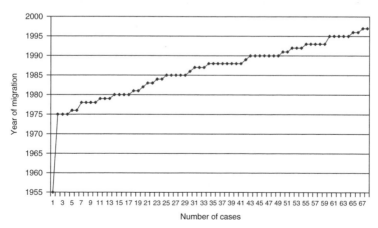

A-5. Grooms' Year of Migration in This Study

year of migration: 9 percent (n = 6/68) migrated on or before the year Saigon fell in 1975; and 28 percent (n = 19/68) migrated in or before 1980, which means that they had been living in the United States for nearly twenty years before returning to Vietnam for marriage in 1999–2000. Nearly three-quarters of the men (n = 50/68) migrated in or before 1990. This means that, in general, the majority of the men had been living in the diaspora for about ten years before they went back to Vietnam for marriage. A little over a quarter of the men (n = 18/68) migrated after 1990, and only 6 percent (n = 4/68) migrated after 1995.

Among the immigrant grooms, 30 percent (n = 21/68) migrated as children. Of those who migrated as children, 40 percent (n = 8/21) migrated without their parents, with roughly half migrating with an adult relative other than a parent, and another half migrating as unaccompanied minors. Among all the immigrant men, 16 percent (n = 11/69) could be considered as part of the "new" second generation, that is, those post-1965 immigrants who migrated at or before the age of twelve. Despite the fact that most of these grooms were relatively long-term immigrants, about 40 percent were not yet citizens of their country of residence.

Discussion

The characteristics of respondents reveal the diversity of the sample. Except for a few cases of Vietnamese or formerly Vietnamese nationals of ethnic Chinese origin who returned to Vietnam for wives, most transpacific husbands and wives in this sample were ethnic Vietnamese. Brides came from both urban Saigon and rural areas, and they married grooms who were primarily concentrated in four core countries of the aging Vietnamese diaspora. Transpacific husbands in this sample came from a total of eight different countries, with 68 percent of them from the United States. Husbands in the United States came from sixteen states. Both transpacific husbands and wives married on average at an older age than the average age of first marriage in their local marriage markets, suggesting that these transpacific brides and grooms were people who, for various reasons, had experienced prolonged single status. Transpacific husbands were on average 5.5 years older than their wives. And except for a few anomalous cases, over 80 percent of husbands were ten or fewer years older than their wives, with 61 percent (n = 42) of the wives five or fewer years younger than husbands. Most transpacific husbands and wives were never-married people at the time of marriage; only a few of the couples were both part of a remarriage market.

Transpacific brides tended to be more educated than their husbands. About 70 percent of the brides had at least a college education, and of these brides, 40 percent had an advanced degree. Although 23 percent of the grooms had a college education, only 11.5 percent of all the grooms earned it after migration, suggesting that transpacific grooms experienced either downward mobility or nonmobility as a result of migration. Most brides and grooms worked for a wage, with 81 percent of the grooms in low-wage jobs and 54 percent of the brides in high-wage jobs, all relative to their local labor markets.

These Vietnamese international arrangements were facilitated by transnational networks that had been sustained over many years after the war, or renewed after 1986, when Vietnam reentered the global economy. Most of the brides had at least one relative living abroad, whereas all the grooms had at least one relative living in Vietnam. The grooms' transnational networks revealed the ways in which these men entered the Vietnamese diaspora. A substantial number of them migrated by themselves, leaving all of their immediate relatives behind, and only a small number of them were able to sponsor their parents after they settled in the host society. All but one groom were born in Vietnam. Grooms varied widely in the year of migration. Nearly three-quarters of them migrated in or before 1990, which means that they had been living in the diaspora for at least ten years before they went back to Vietnam for marriage. A little over a quarter of the men had been living in the diaspora for nearly twenty years before returning; 16 percent can be considered as part of the "new" second generation. Despite the fact that many of the grooms were long-term migrants, 40 percent were not yet citizens of their country of residence.

Nearly all the transpacific brides lived with their parents at the time of marriage, and most of them continued to do so after they married. A few exceptions were women who had moved to live with the grooms' families, especially in cases where grooms' parents were still in Vietnam. These variants of traditional Vietnamese postmarriage household patterns suggest that international married people had begun to employ new and flexible practices of kinship and household arrangements. In traditional patterns of postmarriage patriarchal residential practices, recently married women usually go and live with their husbands' families; yet, in international cases, the husbands were not present in the household. Most of the wives who moved in with their husbands' families did so only temporarily, since they knew they would soon migrate to join their husbands overseas. They often went back and forth to their own parents' households, a practice that symbolizes one of many larger changing meanings of kinship and marriage in the context of the contemporary Vietnamese international marriage market.

Notes

Preface   The Intimate Details of Globalization

1. Although Saigon's name was changed to Ho Chi Minh City when the South surrendered to North Vietnamese military troops in 1975, most people I met in contemporary southern Vietnam still refer to the city as Saigon, or simply *thanh pho* (the city). In this book, I echo their frames of reference by using the name Saigon, and Saigonese to refer to the locals there.
2. I note Ara Wilson's use of the term "intimate economies" to talk about interactions between economic systems and social life. Wilson notes that the use of the plural economies "recognizes that there are different economic systems even within the same society" (2004, 11). I want to call attention to the "global intimate economy" to analyze intimate ties across nation-states.

Introduction   Marriage and Migration in
the New Global Economy

1. Of the 1,122,373 immigrants who entered the United States in 2005, 649,201, or 58 percent, came through various routes of family sponsorship. This is the latest available data from the Annual Statistical Yearbooks of the Office of Immigration Statistics in the United States Department of Homeland Security. These numbers are based on "principal sponsored migrants," which means that individuals entering as "other spouses" (e.g., as the spouse of sons and daughters of U.S. citizens) are not calculated in the overall marriage migrant figure.
2. Precisely 292,741 migrants were marriage migrants in 2005.
3. Between 1975 and 1995, the United States accepted 64 percent of that group; 12 percent went to Australia, and 12 percent to Canada. Among European countries, France received the largest number, although this represents only 3 percent of total resettlements. See Merli 1997.
4. Before 1952, the Vietnamese were not listed as a separate ethnic group in the USINS yearbooks. According to the USINS (1999), there were a total of 335 Vietnamese in the United States between 1951 and 1960, 4,340 between 1961 and 1970, and 13,211 between 1971 and 1974.

5. See, for example, the following works: Allen and Hiller 1985; Baldwin 1982; Caplan, Choy, and Whitmore, 1991; Caplan, Whitmore, and Choy, 1989; Debonis 1995; Freeman 1989, 1995; Gold 1992; Haines 1981; Hein 1995; Hitchcox 1990; Kelly 1977; Kibria 1993; Liu, Lamanna, and Murata 1979; Montero 1979; Rahe et al.1978; Rumbaut 1991; Rumbaut and Ima 1998; Starr and Jones 1983; Thomas 1999; Tollefson 1989; and Zhou and Bankston 1998.

6. These calculations are based on Goodkind's (1997) 1990 data. I simply added ten years to each cohort, though I acknowledge that mortality for either sex as a whole may have caused a shift in sex ratio since 1990.

7. For excellent discussions of these various exclusionary policies, see either Chan 1991 or Espiritu 1997.

8. Among the 18,000 Japanese men on the Pacific Coast States in 1900, there were only 850 women, a sex ratio of 21 to 1. Among Filipinos who arrived in Hawaii from 1907 to 1929, 87 percent were males; on the mainland, almost all Filipino immigrants were single male workers. Of the Koreans who came to Hawaii between 1902 and 1905, only 10 percent were women. Finally, fewer than a dozen women immigrated to the United States before World War II among the approximately 6,400 Asian Indian men who came during this period.

9. For sex-ratio figures, see Espiritu 1997, 20–22.

10. See, for example, the following: Brettell 2006; Portes, Guarnizo, and Landolt 1999; Guarnizo, Portes, and Haller 2003; Kivisto 2001; Levitt 2001a; Levitt and Schiller 2004; Portes 2001, 2003; Glick Schiller 1997, 2005.

11. For example, see the following works: Anthias and Lazaridis 2000; Brettell and deBerjeois 1992; Brettell and Simon 1986; Buijs 1993; Chant 1992; Chant and McIlwaine 1995; Donato 1992; Gamburd 2000; Hondagneu-Sotelo 1994, 2001; Hondagneu-Sotelo and Avila 1997; Morokvasic, Erel, and Shinozaki 2002; Oishi 2005; Parrenas 2001a, 2001b; Pedraza 1991; Phizacklea 1983; Piper and Roces 2003; Romero 1992; Simon and Brettell 1986.

12. I made four subsequent short return visits in the winters of 1997 and 1998 for one month each, and in the summers of 1998 and 1999 for three months each. By the time I got to data analysis and write-up, I had made over twenty-five trips to Vietnam from 1997 to 2006.

13. Various individuals at the Institute had strong ties with many local and state officials, which enabled us to receive names of registered marriages. In the beginning, I insisted on using snowball samples because I felt it would have been easier, given the topic at hand, to obtain a large sample and to interview people I had already known. But my central concern throughout was to obtain proper government permissions for my research project, and in order to obtain those permissions, I needed the Institute to agree with my research

procedures. The process of obtaining these permissions was slow and entailed continual negotiations and inquires. At one point early on, I almost quit, considering that if I did not get to do fieldwork in Vietnam, I could easily get to know couples in the United States in situations where the wives had already migrated overseas to join their husbands. But in the end, the fact that I was prevented from using snowball sampling proved to be an enormous advantage to my project, both in terms of the ease of swiftly recruiting a large number of respondents in a short period of time, and also because of the methodological logic and data analysis that followed.

14. I have changed the names of all rural villages in Vietnam and small towns in the United States. I have kept the real names of all metropolitan areas. I use miles here instead of kilometers, the measurement used by locals in Vietnam, because I will also refer to distances in the United States in the chapters that follow.

15. I note this because some couples did not register their marriages immediately after their weddings, and some never registered at all. Most husbands returned overseas very soon after they got married, staying in Vietnam no more than a month after their weddings. Many of them could not afford to stay away from their overseas jobs for long periods, even when their bosses allowed them to do so.

16. In both sites, all the names of registered international marriages were computerized as well as placed in a handwritten binder. Each binder had names of registered married people spanning at least five years. We were given the liberty to go through the binders or to have the directors of the Department of Justice generate the names for us on their computers. Thus, the process of name selection was completely random, because we were able to choose whichever method we wanted to select the names from the entire universe of the registered international marriages. In the end, I asked the directors of the Department of Justice to computer-generate names of registered marriages in the three previous months (September, October, and November) prior to my arrival in December 1999 for the long stint of fieldwork in Vietnam. I then tallied up the total number of marriages in those three months, divided the total number of marriages by 200 in Saigon and 120 in Se Long for every Nth couple in order to receive 200 names from Saigon and 120 names from Se Long. I selected every fourth name from each of these two lists, with the goal of receiving a sample of 80 marriages.

17. The response rate for the brides was 86 percent (n = 69/80). Of the forty-seven U.S.-based grooms, I contacted twenty-eight in the four U.S. fieldsites, and all participated in the study.

18. I met sixty-six brides and twenty-seven of their family members in the bride phase of research. I did not meet three of the wives who were included in my sample because I discovered that they had already left Vietnam to join their husbands abroad. Two of these

wives emigrated to France, and the third to Australia. I decided, nevertheless, to include the marriages of the three women whom I did not meet in my analysis because interviews with their families who were still in Vietnam gave me extensive information about their marriages.

19. I interviewed twenty-eight grooms and eight of their family members for a total of thirty-six individuals in the groom phase of this project.

20. Of all the interviews I conducted, 60 percent lasted at least two hours, and some took as long as five hours. The rest of the interviews ran about thirty minutes each, most often as follow-up interviews that I usually conducted via recorded phone conversations. Some of the follow-up interviews, especially those with most of the husbands, were done through face-to-face revisits in participants' homes and workplaces.

21. By that time, I had already interviewed several members of each household at least twice, all of whom crossed intergenerational lines, and had established rapport with various family members within each household, although not necessarily with the transpacific wives.

22. The stints of participant observation were largely informal. I kept brief and cursory fieldnotes. I generally dropped by several times a week unannounced and casually engaged in informal conversations with the wives and their families.

23. Generally, transnational split households, even when they were only temporary choices, were rare, and ultimately, migration was the eventual goal for the brides. This may change over time, but during this project, I did not find it to be a significant choice. It was certainly not a typical pattern. In all the transnational split households, I did not find anything significant about their temporary decision not to migrate in terms of how that affected their thoughts and motivations for entering international marriages. I decided not to write a chapter on these couples because even though they told me they wanted to maintain transnational split households, there were plans to migrate eventually. Perhaps a project on return migration might bring out more data telling a different story than I had collected.

24. In the end, there was nothing in my interview data or in my observations of families and couples that led me to believe that any of the couples in my sample were in fake marriages or that the men were there to marry second wives. I do know from fieldwork that there were cases of men who were in fact married overseas and returned to Vietnam for extramarital affairs. But I never heard of a case where these men successfully sponsored marriage migration for their girlfriends or mistresses. This is because if they were married abroad, it was impossible for them to have legal paperwork to show that they were single, rather than married, in order to register their marriages.

And since single status is required to sponsor a spouse, it was impossible for men to sponsor mistresses. Therefore, they would not fall into my sample.

CHAPTER 1   THE GIFT OF MODERNITY

1. To protect the privacy of informants, all names have been changed. And although full Vietnamese names are usually indicated in the order of last, middle, and first names, I will use "American" standards of referencing names since I used this format when I got to know informants.
2. In order to make generational distinctions, I refer to brides and grooms by their first names in this study; and I refer to their elders using proper titles, although when I spoke to these individuals I employed Vietnamese kinship terms, since all titles of address are kinship terms. When it is clearer, I will use first names for elders as well to avoid confusion for the reader.
3. Throughout this book, I will interchangeably use the terms "brides and grooms" with "wives and husbands." When speaking in the third person, the Vietnamese make distinctions between the two sets of terms based on how new marriages are, with "brides and grooms" used for more recently married people. When speaking in the first person, most people use "wives and husbands."
4. The reader will note that Trang's parents have different surnames, Mr. Le and Mrs. Liem, because it is uncommon for women in Vietnam to take their husbands' surname. I have kept this pattern throughout this book so as to maintain the authenticity of identities.
5. I use the term "gender ideology" to mean "beliefs about manhood and womanhood, beliefs that are forged in early childhood and thus anchored to deep emotions" (Hochschild 1989, 15).
6. While I was in the course of doing this research project, the Immigration and Naturalization Service changed its name to the U.S. Citizenship and Immigration Services.
7. I would like to thank Jill Grigsby for helping me see this line of argument.

CHAPTER 5   MONEY

1. For an explanation of how I divided these different levels of wage earners, please refer to the characteristics of the sample in Appendix B.

CHAPTER 6   THE TWO UNMARRIAGEABLES

1. I refer to men as both "low-wage workers" and "undereducated" men. The brides are "highly educated" women compared to most

women in Vietnam, meaning that they all have at least a college degree and many have advanced degrees. Most of them, though not all, come from solidly middle-class Vietnamese backgrounds. For this reason, I refer to the women mostly as highly educated, rather than as middle-class women.

2. When low-wage men travel abroad in search of spouses, many are unlikely to claim they work in low-wage jobs. However, I believe that most of the men in my study told their wives, through match-makers and go-betweens, that they work in low-wage jobs. Thus, the 55 percent calculation of low-wage men married to highly educated women is based on information provided by the brides and their families, and interviews with some of the grooms of the those brides. Among the grooms I interviewed, I did not find any misrepresentations when I compared their answers to the brides' stories. If anything, grooms are more likely to claim to their future wives that they work in high-wage, rather than low-wage, jobs. Thus, even though I estimate that 80 percent of the grooms in my study are low-wage workers, that number may, in fact, be higher if they told their wives they work in high-wage rather than low-wage jobs.

Chapter 7   The Highly Marriageables

1. The reader will note that Joe does not share the same surname as his mother; this is because it is uncommon for women in Vietnam to take their husbands' surname. Children generally take their father's surname. I have kept this pattern throughout to maintain the authenticity of identities.

2. Indeed, Mrs. Bui's anxiety echoed the concerns that U.S. immigration officials had pertaining to foreign wives of American citizens, which prompted the Marriage Fraud Amendment Acts of 1986. This act allowed the Immigration and Naturalization Service to impose conditional permanent resident status after the migration of foreign brides. This act stipulated that an immigrant spouse could be deported if she left the marriage before two years elapsed. As Constable (2003) notes, although immigration laws are theoretically gender neutral, legal scholars have argued that the Marriage Fraud Act were fueled by concerns surrounding foreign brides, particularly mail-order brides from Asia.

References

Abu-Lughod, Lila. 1998. *Remaking Women: Feminism and Modernity in the Middle East*. Princeton: Princeton University Press.

Allen, Rebecca, and Harry Hiller. 1985. "The Social Organization of Migration: An Analysis of the Uprooting and Flight of Vietnamese Refugees." *International Migration Review* 23(4): 439–451.

Alonso, Ana Maria. 1994. "The Politics of Space, Time and Substance: State Formation, Nationalism, and Ethnicity." *Annual Review of Anthropology* 23: 379–405.

Anderson, Wanni W., and Robert G. Lee. 2005. "Asian American Displacements." Pp. 3–22 in *Displacements and Diasporas: Asians in the Americas*, edited by W. W. Anderson and R. G. Lee. New Brunswick: Rutgers University Press.

Anthias, Floya, and Gabriella Lazaridis. 2000. *Gender and Migration in Southern Europe: Women on the Move*. Oxford: Berg.

Appadurai, Arjun. 1985. "Gratitude as a Social Mode in South India." *Ethos* 13(3): 236–245.

———. 1991. "Global Ethnoscapes: Notes and Queries for a Transnational Anthropology." Pp. 191–210 in *Recapturing Anthropology: Working in the Present*, edited by R. Fox. Santa Fe, N.M.: School of American Research Press.

———. 1996. *Modernity at Large: Cultural Dimensions of Globalization*. Minneapolis: University of Minnesota Press.

Baldwin, Beth C. 1982. *Capturing the Change: The Impact of Indochinese Refugees in Orange County, Challenges and Opportunities*. Santa Ana, Cal.: Immigration and Refugee Planning Center.

Balzani, Marzia. 2006. "Transnational Marriage among Ahmadi Muslims in the UK." *Global Networks* 6(4): 345–355.

Basch, Linda, Nina Glick Schiller, and Christina Szanton Blanc. 1994. *Nations Unbound: Transnational Projects, Postcolonial Predicaments, and Deterritorialized Nation-States*. Amsterdam: Gordon and Breach.

Bashi, Vilna Francine. 2007. *Survival of the Knitted: Immigrant Social Networks in a Stratified World*. Stanford: Stanford University Press.

Belanger, Daniele. 2000. "Regional Differences in Household Composition and Family Formation Patterns in Vietnam." *Journal of Comparative Family Studies* 31(2): 171–189.

Belanger, Daniele, and Khuat Thu Hong. 1996. "Marriage and the Family in Urban North Vietnam, 1965–1993." *Journal of Population* 2(1): 83–112.

Bernard, Jessie. 1972. *The Future of Marriage.* New York: World Publishing.

Bodnar, John, Roger Simon, and Michael P. Weber. 1982. *Lives of Their Own: Blacks, Italians, and Poles in Pittsburgh, 1900–1960.* Urbana: University of Illinois Press.

Booth, Alan, Ann C. Crouter, and Nancy Landale. 1997. *Immigration and the Family: Research and Policy on U.S. Immigrants.* Mahwah, N.J.: Lawrence Erlbaum Associates.

Bourdieu, Pierre. 1977. *Outline of a Theory of Practice.* Cambridge: Cambridge University Press.

———. 1980. *The Logic of Practice.* Stanford: Stanford University Press.

———. 1984. *Distinction: A Social Critique of the Judgment of Taste.* Cambridge: Harvard University Press.

———. 1986. "The Forms of Capital." Pp. 241–258 in *Handbook of Theory and Research for the Sociology of Education,* edited by John G. Richardson. New York: Greenwood.

Bourdieu, Pierre, and Loic Wacquant. 1992. *An Invitation to Sociology.* Chicago: University of Chicago Press.

Brennan, Denise. 2004. *What's Love Got to Do with It?: Transnational Desires and Sex Tourism in the Dominican Republic.* Durham: Duke University Press.

Brettell, Caroline B. 2006. "Global Spaces/Local Spaces: Transnationalism, Diaspora, and the Meaning of Home." *Identities* 13(4): 327–334.

Brettell, Caroline B., and Patricia A. deBerjeois. 1992. "Anthropology and the Study of Immigrant Women." Pp. 41–64 in *Seeking Common Ground: Multidisciplinary Studies of Immigrant Women in the United States,* edited by D. Gabaccia. Westport, Conn.: Greenwood.

Brettell, Caroline B., and Rita J. Simon. 1986. "Immigrant Women: An Introduction." Pp. 3–21 in *International Migration: The Female Experience,* edited by R. J. Simon and C. B. Brettell. Totowa, N.J.: Rowman and Allanheld.

Buijs, Gina. 1993. *Migrant Women: Crossing Boundaries and Changing Identities.* Oxford: Berg.

Caplan, Nathan, Marcella H. Choy, and John K. Whitmore. 1991. *Children of the Boat People: A Study of Educational Success.* Ann Arbor: University of Michigan Press.

Caplan, Nathan, John K. Whitmore, and Marcella H. Choy. 1989. *The Boat People and Achievement in America: A Study of Family Life, Hard Work, and Cultural Values*. Ann Arbor: University of Michigan Press.

Carrigan, Tim, Bob Connell, and John Lee. 1985. "Toward a New Sociology of Masculinity." *Theory and Society* 14(5): 551–604.

Chan, Sucheng. 1991. *Asian Americans: An Interpretive History*. London: Twayne.

Chant, Sylvia. 1992. *Gender and Migration in Developing Countries*. London: Behaven.

Chant, Sylvia, and Cathy McIlwaine. 1995. *Women of a Lesser Cost: Female Labour, Foreign Exchange, and Philippine Development*. London: Pluto.

Charsley, Katharine. 2005. "Unhappy Husbands: Masculinity and Migration in Transnational Pakistani Marriages." *Journal of the Royal Anthropological Institute* 11(1): 85–105.

———. 2006. "Risk and Ritual: The Protection of British Pakistani Women in Transnational Marriage." *Journal of Ethnic and Migration Studies* 32(7): 1169–1187.

Charsley, Katharine, and Alison Shaw. 2006. "South Asian Transnational Marriages in Comparative Perspective." *Global Networks* 6(4): 331–344.

Chatterjee, Partha. 1993. *The Nation and Its Fragments: Colonial and Postcolonial Histories*. Princeton: Princeton University Press.

Chen, Anthony S. 1999. "Lives at the Center of the Periphery, Lives at the Periphery of the Center." *Gender & Society* 13(5): 584–607.

Clark, Candace. 1987. "Sympathy Biography and Sympathy Margin." *American Journal of Sociology* 93(2): 290–321.

———. 1997. *Misery and Company*. Chicago: University of Chicago Press.

Connell, R. W. 1995. *Masculinities*. Berkeley: University of California Press.

Constable, Nicole. 2003. *Romance on a Global Stage: Pen Pals, Virtual Ethnography, and "Mail-Order" Marriages*. Berkeley: University of California Press.

———. 2005. *Cross-Border Marriages: Gender and Mobility in Transnational Asia*. Philadelphia: University of Pennsylvania Press.

Curran, Sara R., Steven Shafer, Katharine M. Donato, and Filiz Garip. 2006. "Mapping Gender in Migration in Sociological Scholarship: Is It Segregation or Integration?" *International Migration Review* 40(1): 199–223.

Dalaker, Joseph. 2001. *Poverty in the United States: 2000*. U.S. Census Bureau, Current Population Reports, Series P60–214. Washington, D.C.: U.S. Government Printing Office.

Debonis, Steven. 1995. *Children of the Enemy: Oral Histories of Vietnamese Amerasians and Their Mothers*. Jefferson, N.C.: McFarland.

Donato, Katharine M. 1992. "Understanding U.S. Immigration: Why Some Countries Send Women and Others Send Men." Pp. 159–184 in *Seeking Common Ground: Multidisciplinary Studies of Immigrant Women in the United States*, edited by D. Gabaccia. Westport, Conn.: Praeger.

Donato, Katharine M., Donna Gabaccia, Jennifer Holdaway, Martin Manalansan, and Patricia R. Pessar. 2006. "A Glass Half Full? Gender in Migration Studies." *International Migration Review* 40(1): 3–26.

Ebashi, Masahiko. 1997. "The Economic Take-Off." Pp. 37–65 in *Vietnam Joins the World*, edited by J. Morley and M. Nishihara. Armonk, N.Y.: M. E. Sharpe.

Ehrenreich, Barbara. 2001. *Nickel and Dimed: On Not Getting by in America*. New York: Metropolitan Books.

Enloe, Cynthia. 2000. *Bananas, Beaches, and Bases*. Berkeley: University of California Press.

Espiritu, Yen Le. 1997. *Asian American Women and Men: Labor, Laws and Love*. Thousand Oaks, Cal.: Sage.

———. 1999. "Gender and Labor in Asian Immigrant Families." *American Behavioral Scientist* 42(4): 628–647.

———. 2003. *Home Bound: Filipino American Lives across Cultures, Communities, and Countries*. Berkeley: University of California Press.

Farrell, Warren. 1975. *The Liberated Man*. New York: Random House.

Fforde, Adam, and Stefan de Vylder. 1996. *From Planet to Markets: The Economic Transition in Vietnam*. Boulder, Col.: Westview.

Freeman, James M. 1989. *Hearts of Sorrow: Vietnamese American Lives*. Stanford: Stanford University Press.

———. 1995. *Changing Identities: Vietnamese Americans, 1975–1995*. Boston: Allyn and Bacon.

Gamburd, Michele Ruth. 2000. *The Kitchen Spoon's Handle: Transnationalism and Sri Lanka's Migrant Housemaids*. Ithaca: Cornell University Press.

Glaser, Barney G., and Anselm L. Strauss. 1967. *The Discovery of Grounded Theory: Strategies for Qualitative Research*. New York: Aldine de Gruyter.

Glassner, Barry, and Rosanna Hertz. 2003. *Our Studies, Ourselves: Sociologists' Lives and Work*. Oxford: Oxford University Press.

Glenn, Evelyn Nakano. 1983. "Split Household, Small Producer and Dual Wage Earner: An Analysis of Chinese-American Family Strategies." *Journal of Marriage and Family* 45(1): 35–46.

———. 1986. *Issei, Nisei, War Bride: Three Generations of Japanese-American Women in Domestic Service*. Philadelphia: Temple University Press.

Glick Schiller, Nina. 1997. "The Situation of Transnational Studies." *Identities* 4(2): 155–166.

————. 2005. "Transnational Social Fields and Imperialism." *Anthropological Theory* 5(4): 439–461.

Glick Schiller, Nina, Linda Basch, and Cristina Blanc-Szanton. 1992. *Towards a Transnational Perspective on Migration: Race, Class, Ethnicity, and Nationalism Reconsidered.* New York: New York Academy of Sciences.

Glick Schiller, Nina, and Georges Fouron. 1998. "Transnational Lives and National Identities: The Identity Politics of Haitian Immigrants." Pp. 130–161 in *Transnationalism from Below*, edited by M. P. Smith and L. E. Guarnizo. New Brunswick, N.J.: Transaction.

Glodava, Mila, and Richard Onizuka. 1994. *Mail-Order Brides: Women for Sale.* Fort Collins, Col: Alaken.

Gold, Steven J. 1992. *Refugee Communities: A Comparative Field Study.* Newbury Park, Cal.: Sage.

Goldring, Luin. 1998. "The Power of Status in Transnational Social Fields." Pp. 165–195 in *Transnationalism from Below*, edited by M. P. Smith and L. E. Guarnizo. New Brunswick, N.J.: Transaction.

————. 2003. "Gender, Status, and the State in Transnational Spaces." Pp. 341–358 in *Gender and U.S. Immigration: Contemporary Trends*, edited by P. Hondagneu-Sotelo. Berkeley: University of California Press.

Goodkind, Daniel. 1997. "The Vietnamese Double Marriage Squeeze." *International Migration Review* 31(1): 108–128.

Gouldner, Alvin W. 1960. "The Norm of Reciprocity: A Preliminary Statement." *American Sociological Review* 25(2): 161–178.

Grasmuck, Sherri, and Patricia Pessar. 1991. *Between Two Islands: Dominican International Migration.* Berkeley: University of California Press.

Grewal, Inderpal, and Caren Kaplan. 1994. *Scattered Hegemonies: Postmodernity and Transnational Feminist Practices.* Minneapolis: University of Minnesota Press.

Guarnizo, Luis E. 1992. "'Los Dominicanyorks': The Making of a Binational Society." Pp. 70–86 in *Towards a Transnational Perspective on Migration: Race, Class, Ethnicity, and Nationalism*, edited by N. Glick Schiller, L. Basch, and C. Blanc-Szanton. New York: Annals of the New York Academy of Sciences.

————. 1997. "The Emergence of a Transnational Social Formation and the Mirage of Return Migration among Dominican Transmigrants." *Identities: Global Studies in Culture and Power* 4(2): 281–322.

Guarnizo, Luis E., Alejandro Portes, and William Haller. 2003. "Assimilation and Transnationalism: Determinants of Transnational Political Action among Contemporary Migrants." *American Journal of Sociology* 108(6): 1211–1248.

Guarnizo, Luis E., and Michael Peter Smith. 1998. "The Location of Transnationalism." Pp. 3–34 in *Transnationalism from Below*, edited by M. P. Smith and L. E. Guarnizo. New Brunswick, N.J.: Transaction.

Gubrium, Jaber F. 1990. *What Is Family?* Mountain View, Cal.: Mayfield.

Gupta, Akhil, and James Ferguson. 1997. *Culture, Power, Place: Explorations in Critical Anthropology*. Durham: Duke University Press.

Gutek, Barbara A. 1995. *The Dynamics of Service*. San Francisco: Jossey-Bass.

Guttentag, Marcia, and Paul F. Secord. 1983. *Too Many Women?: The Sex Ratio Question*. Beverly Hills, Cal.: Sage.

Haines, David W. 1981. *Refugee Settlement in the United States: An Annotated Bibliography on the Adjustment of Cuban, Soviet, and Southeast Asian Refugees*. Washington, D.C.: Office of Refugee Resettlement, Department of Health and Human Services.

Hall, John. 1992. "The Capital(s) of Cultures: A Nonholistic Approach to Status, Situations, Class, Gender, and Ethnicity." Pp. 257–289 in *Cultivating Differences: Symbolic Boundaries and the Making of Inequalities*, edited by M. Lamont and M. Fournier. Chicago: University of Chicago Press.

Han, Vo Xuan, and Roger Baumgarte. 2000. "Economic Reform, Private Sector Development, and the Business Environment in Vietnam." *Comparative Economic Studies* 42(3): 1–30.

Handlin, Oscar. 1951. *The Uprooted*. Boston: Little, Brown.

Hein, Jeremy. 1995. *From Vietnam, Laos, and Cambodia: A Refugee Experience in the United States*. New York: Twayne.

Hiebert, Murray. 1996. *Chasing the Tigers: A Portrait of the New Vietnam*. New York: Kodansha International.

Hirschman, Charles, and Vu Manh Loi. 1996. "Family and Household Structures in Vietnam: Some Glimpses from a Recent Survey." *Pacific Affairs* 69(2): 229–249.

Hitchcox, Linda. 1990. *Vietnamese Refugees in Southeast Asian Camps*. New York: St. Martin's.

Hite, Shere. 1988. *Women and Love*. New York: Knopf.

Hochschild, Arlie Russell. 1983. *The Managed Heart: Commercialization of Human Feeling*. Berkeley: University of California Press.

———. 1994. "The Commercial Spirit of Intimate Life and the Abduction of Feminism: Signs from Women's Advice Books." *Theory, Culture, & Society* 11(2): 1–24.

Hochschild, Arlie Russell, with Anne Machung. 1989. *The Second Shift: Working Parents and the Revolution at Home*. New York: Viking.

Hondagneu-Sotelo, Pierrette. 1994. *Gendered Transitions: Mexican Experiences of Immigration*. Berkeley: University of California Press.

———. 2001. *Domestica: Immigrant Workers Cleaning and Caring in the Shadows of Affluence*. Berkeley: University of California Press.

———. 2003. *Gender and U.S. Immigration: Contemporary Trends*. Berkeley: University of California Press.

Hondagneu-Sotelo, Pierrette, and Ernestine Avila. 1997. "'I'm Here, but I'm There': The Meanings of Latina Transnational Motherhood." *Gender & Society* 11(5): 548–571.

Hong, Vu Thi, Le Van Thanh, and Troung Si Anh. 1996. *Migration, Human Resources, Employment and Urbanization in Ho Chi Minh City.* Hanoi: National Political Publishing House.

Houstoun, Marion, Roger Kramer, and Joan Mackin Barrett. 1984. "Female Predominance in Immigration to the Unites States since 1930: A First Look." *International Migration Review* 18(4): 902–925.

Howe, Irvin. 1976. *World of Our Fathers.* New York: Simon & Schuster.

Jana, Reena. 2000. "Arranged Marriages, Minus the Parents: For Some South Asians, Matrimonial Sites Both Honor and Subvert Tradition." *New York Times,* August 17, G1

Jones-Correa, Michael. 1998a. *Between Two Nations: The Political Predicament of Latinos in New York City.* Ithaca: Cornell University Press.

———. 1998b. "Different Paths: Gender, Immigration and Political Participation." *International Migration Review* 32(2): 326–349.

Kalmijn, Matthijs. 1998. "Intermarriage and Homogamy: Causes, Patterns, Trends." *Annual Review of Sociology* 24: 395–421.

Kandiyoti, Deniz. 1988. "Bargaining with Patriarchy." *Gender & Society* 2(3): 274–290.

Katrak, Ketu. 1996. "South Asian American Writers: Geography and Memory." *Amerasia Journal* 22(3): 121–138.

Keenan, Faith. 1997. "What Economic Crisis: Vietnam Halts Economic Reforms." *Far Eastern Economic Review* 160(1): 26–29.

Kelly, Gail Paradise. 1977. *From Vietnam to America: A Chronicle of the Vietnamese Immigration to the United States.* Boulder, Col.: Westview.

Kelsky, Karen. 2001. *Women on the Verge: Japanese Women, Western Dreams.* Durham: Duke University Press.

Kempadoo, Kamala. 1999. "Slavery or Work? Reconceptualizing Third World Prostitution." *Positions* 7(1): 225–237.

———. 2004. *Sexing the Caribbean: Gender, Race, and Sexual Labor.* New York: Routledge.

Kibria, Nazli. 1993. *Family Tightrope: The Changing Lives of Vietnamese Americans.* Princeton: Princeton University Press.

———. 2002. *Becoming Asian-American: Second Generation Chinese and Korean American Identities.* Baltimore: Johns Hopkins University Press.

Kivisto, Peter. 2001. "Theorizing Transnational Immigration: A Critical Review of Current Efforts." *Ethnic and Racial Studies* 24(4): 549–577.

Komter, Aafke, and Wilma Vollebergh. 1997. "Gift Giving and the Emotional Significance of Family and Friends." *Journal of Marriage and the Family* 59(3): 747–757.

Kondo, Dorinne. 1996. "The Narrative Production of 'Home' Community, and Political Identity of Asian American Theatre." Pp. 97–117 in *Displacement, Diaspora, and Geographies of Identity*, edited by S. Lavie and T. Swedenburg. Durham: Duke University Press.

Lamont, Michele. 1992. *Money, Morals, and Manners: The Culture of the French and the American Upper-Middle Class*. Chicago: University of Chicago Press.

Leonard, Jack, and Mai Tran. 2000a. "Agents Target Little Saigon Crime Groups." *Los Angeles Times*, October 7, A–1.

———. 2000b. "Probes Take Aim at Organized Crime in Little Saigon; Crackdown: Numerous Agencies Target Gambling, Drug Sales, Counterfeit Labels and Credit Card Scams." *Los Angeles Times*, October 7, B–7.

Lévi-Strauss, Claude. 1957. "The Principle of Reciprocity." Pp. 61–70 in *Sociological Theory: A Book of Readings*, edited by L. A. Coser and B. Rosenberg. New York: Macmillan.

Levitt, Peggy. 1998. "Social Remittances: Migration Driven Local-Level Forms of Cultural Diffusion." *International Migration Review* 32(14): 926–948.

———. 2001a. "Transnational Migration: Taking Stock and Future Directions." *Global Networks* 1(3): 195–216.

———. 2001b. *The Transnational Villagers*. Berkeley: University of California Press.

Levitt, Peggy, and Nina Glick Schiller. 2004. "Conceptualizing Simultaneity: A Transnational Social Field Perspective on Society." *International Migration Review* 38(3): 1002–1039.

Liao, Cailian, and Tim B. Heaton. 1992. "Divorce Trends and Differentials in China." *Journal of Comparative Family Studies* 23(3): 413–429.

Liu, William T., Maryanne Lamanna, and Alice Murata. 1979. *Transition to Nowhere: Vietnamese Refugees in America*. Nashville, Tenn.: Charter House.

Long, Lynellyn D. 2004. "Viet Kieu on a Fast Track Back." Pp. 65–89 in *Coming Home?: Refugees, Migrants, and Those Who Stayed Behind*, edited by E. Oxfeld and L. D. Long. Philadelphia: University of Pennsylvania Press.

Lowe, Lisa. 1996. *Immigrant Acts: On Asian American Cultural Politics*. Durham: Duke University Press.

Luong, Hy V. 1990. *Discursive Practices and Linguistic Meanings: The Vietnamese System of Personal Reference*. Amsterdam: John Benjamins.

Luong, Hy Van. 1992. *Revolution in the Village: Tradition and Transformation in North Vietnam, 1925–1988*. Honolulu: University of Hawaii Press.

Luu, Dai Thuyet, and Nguyen Chi Dung. 1995. "Su Bien Doi Co Cau Xa Hoi Giai Cap O Nuoc Ta Hien Nay [The Change in Social Class Structure in Our Country]." Pp. 5–21 in *Situation and Development Trend: Social Structure in Our Country in This Period*, edited by D. N. Phuong. Hanoi: Agricultural Publishing House.

Mahler, Sarah J., and Patricia R. Pessar. 2001. "Gendered Geographies of Power: Analyzing Gender across Transnational Spaces." *Identities: Global Studies in Culture and Power* 7(4): 441–459.

———. 2006. "Gender Matters: Ethnographers Bring Gender from the Periphery toward the Core of Migration Studies." *International Migration Review* 40(1): 27–63.

Maira, Sunaina Marr. 2002. *Desis in the House: Indian American Youth Culture in New York City*. Philadelphia: Temple University Press.

Malarney, Shaun Kingsley. 1996. "The Limits of 'State Functionalism' and the Reconstruction of Funerary Ritual in Contemporary Northern Vietnam." *American Ethnologist* 23(3): 540–560.

Malinowski, Bronislaw. 1959. *Crime and Custom in Savage Society*. Paterson, N.J.: Littlefield Adams.

Marosi, Richard, and Mai Tran. 2000. "Little Saigon Raids Dismantle Crime Ring, Authorities Say; Probe: Asian Syndicate Supplied Most Illegal Gambling Machines in Orange County." *Los Angeles Times*, September 29, B–3.

Marr, David. 1981. *Vietnamese Tradition on Trial 1920–45*. Berkeley: University of California Press.

———. 1997. "Vietnamese Youth in the 1990s." *Vietnam Review* 2 (Spring/Summer): 289–374.

Massey, Doreen, and Pat Jess. 1995. *A Place in the World: Places, Cultures, and Globalization*. New York: Oxford University Press.

Massey, Douglas, Rafael Alarcon, Jorge Durand, and Humberto Gonzalez. 1987. *Return to Aztlan*. Berkeley: University of California Press.

Mauss, Marcel. 2000. *The Gift: The Form and Reason for Exchange in Archaic Societies*. New York: W. W. Norton.

Merli, Giovanna M. 1997. "Estimation of International Migration for Vietnam 1979–1989." Working Paper Series No. 97–04. Seattle: Center for Studies in Demography and Ecology, University of Washington.

Merton, Robert K. 1967. *Social Theory and Social Structure*. New York: Free Press.

———. 1972. "Insiders and Outsiders: A Chapter in the Sociology of Knowledge." *American Journal of Sociology* 78(1): 8–47.

Montero, Darrel. 1979. *Vietnamese Americans: Patterns of Resettlement and Socioeconomic Adaptation in the United States*. Boulder, Col.: Westview.

Moore, Henrietta. 1994. *A Passion for Difference: Essays in Anthropology and Gender*. Bloomington: Indiana University Press.

Moore, Molly. 1994. "Changing India, Wedded to Tradition; Arranged Marriages Persist with '90's Twists." *Washington Post*, October 8.

Morley, James W., and Masashi Nishihara. 1997a. *Vietnam Joins the World*. Armonk, N.Y.: M. E. Sharpe.

———. 1997b. "Vietnam Joins the World." Pp. 3–14 in *Vietnam Joins the World*, edited by J. W. Morley and M. Nishihara. Armonk, N.Y.: M. E. Sharpe.

Morokvasic, Mirjana, Umut Erel, and Kyoko Shinozaki. 2002. *Crossing Borders and Shifting Boundaries*. Vol. 1. *Gender on the Move*. Opladen, Germany: Leske & Budrich.

Murray, Geoffrey. 1997. *Vietnam: Dawn of a New Market*. New York: St. Martin's Press.

Nadar, Laura. 1986. "From Anguish to Exultation." Pp. 95–118 in *Women in the Field: Anthropological Experiences*, edited by P. Golde. Berkeley: University of California Press.

Narayan, Kirin. 1993. "How Native Is the 'Native Anthropologist'?" *American Anthropologist* 95(3): 671–686.

Narayan, Shoba. 1995. "When Life's Partner Comes Pre-Chosen." *New York Times*, May 4.

Nguyen, Bich Thuan, and Mandy Thomas. 2004. "Young Women and Emergent Postsocialist Sensibilities in Contemporary Vietnam." *Asian Studies Review* 28(2): 133–149.

Nguyen, Hong 2002. "*Viet Kieu* Remittances Set to Top \$2 Billion Target." *Vietnam Investment Review*, December 9, 2002.

Nguyen, Huu Minh. 1997. "Age at First Marriage in Vietnam and Its Determinants." *Asia-Pacific Population Journal* 12(2): 49–74.

Nguyen, Khac Vien, and Ngoc Hu. 1998. *From Saigon to Ho Chi Minh City: A Path of 300 Years*. Hanoi: Gioi Publishers.

Oishi, Nana. 2005. *Women in Motion: Globalization, State Policies, and Labor Migration in Asia*. Stanford: Stanford University Press.

Ong, Aihwa. 1999. *Flexible Citizenship: The Cultural Logics of Transnationality*. Durham: Duke University Press.

Ong, Paul, and John M. Liu. 1994. "U.S. Immigration Policies and Asian Americans." Pp. 45–73 in *The New Asian Immigration in Los Angeles and Global Restructuring*, edited by P. Ong, E. Bonacich, and L. Cheng. Philadelphia: Temple University Press.

Ortner, Sherry B. 1996. *Making Gender: The Politics and Erotics of Culture*. Boston: Beacon.

Packard, Le Anh Tu. 1999. "Asian American Economic Engagement: Vietnam Case Study." Pp. 79–108 in *Across the Pacific: Asian Americans and Globalization*, edited by E. Hu-Dehart. Philadelphia: Temple University Press.

Paddock, Richard C., and Lily Dizon. 1991. "3 Vietnamese Brothers in Shoot-out Led Troubled Lives." *Los Angeles Times*, April 15.

Park, Lisa Sun-Hee. 2005. *Consuming Citizenship: Children of Asian Immigrant Entrepreneurs*. Stanford: Stanford University Press.

Parrenas, Rhacel Salazar. 2001a. "Mothering from a Distance: Emotions, Gender, and Inter-Generational Relations in Filipino Transnational Families." *Feminist Studies* 27(2): 361–390.

———. 2001b. *Servants of Globalization: Women, Migration, and Domestic Work*. Stanford: Stanford University Press.

Pedraza, Silvia. 1991. "Women and Migration: The Social Consequences of Gender." *Annual Review of Sociology* 17: 303–325.

Pessar, Patricia R., and Sarah J. Mahler. 2003. "Transnational Migration: Bringing Gender In." *International Migration Review* 37(3): 812–846.

Pflugfelder, Gregory. 1999. *Cartographies of Desire: Male to Male Sexuality in Japanese Discourse, 1600–1950*. Berkeley: University of California Press.

Phizacklea, A. 1983. *One Way Ticket: Migration and Female Labour*. London: Routledge & Kegan Paul.

Pierre, Andrew J. 2000. "Vietnam's Contradictions." *Foreign Affairs* 79(6): 69–86.

Piore, Michael J. 1979. *Birds of Passage: Migrant Labor in Industrial Society*. Cambridge: Cambridge University Press.

Piper, Nicola, and Mina Roces. 2003. *Wife or Worker: Asian Women and Migration*. Lanham, Md.: Rowman & Littlefield.

Portes, Alejandro. 2001. "Introduction: The Debates and Significance of Immigrant Transnationalism." *Global Networks* 1(3): 181–193.

———. 2003. "Conclusion: Theoretical Convergencies and Empirical Evidence in the Study of Immigrant Transnationalism." *International Migration Review* 37(3): 874–892.

Portes, Alejandro, Luis E. Guarnizo, and Patricia Landolt. 1999. "The Study of Transnationalism: Pitfalls and Promise of an Emergent Research Field." *Ethnic and Racial Studies* 22(2): 217–237.

Portes, Alejandro, and Dag McLeod. 1996. "Educational Progress of Children of Immigrants: The Roles of Class, Ethnicity, and School Context." *Sociology of Education* 69(4): 255–275.

Povinelli, Elizabeth A., and George Chauncey. 1999. "Thinking Sexuality Transnationally: An Introduction." *Journal of Lesbian and Gay Studies* 5(4): 439–450.

Pyke, Karen. 2000. "'The Normal American Family' as an Interpretive Structure of Family Life among Grown Children of Korean and Vietnamese Immigrants." *Journal of Marriage and the Family* 62(1): 240–255.

Rahe, Richard H., John G. Looney, Harold W. Ward, Tran Minh Tung, and William T. Liu. 1978. "Psychiatric Consultation in a Vietnamese Refugee Camp." *American Journal of Psychiatry* 132(2): 185–190.

Rambo, A. Terry. 1973. *A Comparison of Peasant Social Systems of Northern and Southern Viet Nam: A Study of Ecological Adaptation, Social Succession, and Cultural Evolution.* Carbondale: Southern Illinois University Press.

Romero, Mary. 1992. *Maid in the U.S.A.* New York: Routledge.

Rubin, Lillian Breslow. 1976. *Worlds of Pain: Life in the Working-Class Family.* New York: Basic Books.

———. 1994. *Families on the Fault Line: America's Working Class Speaks about the Family, the Economy, Race, and Ethnicity.* New York: Harper Perennial.

Rumbaut, Ruben G. 1991. "The Agony of Exile: A Study of the Migration and Adaptation of Indochinese Refugee Adults and Children." Pp. 53–91 in *Refugee Children: Theory, Research, and Services,* edited by F. L. Ahearn and J. L. Athey. Baltimore: Johns Hopkins University Press.

———. 1997. "Ties That Bind: Immigration and Immigrant Families in the United States." Pp. 3–46 in *Immigration and the Family: Research and Policy on U.S. Immigrants,* edited by A. Booth, A. C. Crouter, and N. Landale. Mahwah, N.J.: Lawrence Erlbaum Associates.

Rumbaut, Ruben G., and Kenji Ima. 1998. *Between Two Worlds: Southeast Asian Refugee Youth in America.* Boulder, Col.: Perseus Books.

Russell, Sharon Stanton. 1986. "Remittances from International Migration: A Review in Perspective." *World Development* 14(6): 677–696.

Rydstrom, Helle. 2003. *Embodying Morality.* Honolulu: University of Hawaii Press.

Saigon: 20 Years after Liberation. 1995. Hanoi: Gioi Publishers.

Sakamoto, Arthur, and Meichu D. Chen. 1991. "Inequality and Attainment in a Dual Labor Market." *American Sociological Review* 56(3): 295–308.

Saltz, Ira S. 1995. "Income Distribution in the Third World: Its Estimation via Proxy Data." *American Journal of Economics and Sociology* 54(1): 15–31.

Sarker, Sonita, and Esha Niyogi De. 2002. "Introduction: Marking Times and Territories." Pp.1–31 in *Trans-Status Subjects: Gender in the Globalization of South and Southeast Asia,* edited by S. Sarker and E. N. De. Durham: Duke University Press.

Schaeffer-Grabiel, Felicity. 2004. "Cyberbrides and Global Imaginaries." *Space and Culture* 7(1): 33–48.

Schwartz, Barry. 1967. "The Social Psychology of the Gift." *American Journal of Sociology* 73(1): 1–11.

Schwartz, Pepper. 1995. *Love between Equals: How Peer Marriage Really Works*. New York: Free Press.

Sidel, Mark. 1999. "Vietnam in 1998: Reform Confronts the Regional Crisis." *Asian Survey* 39(1): 89–90.

Simmel, Georg. 1950. "Faithfulness and Gratitude." Pp. 379–396 in *The Sociology of Georg Simmel*, edited by K. H. Wolff. New York: Free Press.

———. 1996. "Faithfulness and Gratitude." Pp. 39–48 in *The Gift: An Interdisciplinary Perspective*, edited by A. E. Komter. Amsterdam: Amsterdam University Press.

Simon, Rita James, and Caroline Brettell. 1986. *International Migration: The Female Experience*. Totowa, N.J.: Rowman & Allanheld.

Sinke, Suzanne. 1999. "Migration for Labor, Migration for Love: Marriage and Family Formation across Borders." *OAH Magazine of History* (Fall): 17–27.

Sinke, Suzanne, and Stephen Gross. 1992. "The International Marriage Market and the Sphere of Social Reproduction: A German Case Study." Pp. 67–88 in *Seeking Common Ground: Multidisciplinary Studies of Immigrant Women in the United States*, edited by D. Gabaccia. Westport, Conn.: Praeger.

Siu, Lok C. D. 2005. *Memories of a Future Home*. Stanford: Stanford University Press.

Skinner, Kenneth A. 1980. "Vietnamese in America: Diversity in Adaptation." *California Sociologist* 3(2): 103–124.

Smith, Robert. 1998. "Transnational Localities: Community, Technology and Politics of Membership within the Context of Mexico and U.S. Migration." Pp. 196–238 in *Transnationalism from Below*, edited by M. P. Smith and L. E. Guarnizo. New Brunswick, N.J.: Transaction.

———. 2006. *Mexican New York: Transnational Lives of New Immigrants*. Berkeley: University of California Press.

Sofranko, A. J., and Khan Idris. 1999. "Use of Overseas Migrants' Remittances to the Extended Family for Business Investment: A Research Note." *Rural Sociology* 64(3): 464–481.

Starr, Paul D., and W. Jones Jr. 1983. *Indochinese Refugees in America: Problems of Adaptation and Assimilation*. Durham: Duke University Press.

Suzuki, Nobue. 2003. "Of Love and the Marriage Market: Masculinity Politics and Filipina-Japanese Marriages in Japan." Pp. 91–108 in *Men and Masculinities in Contemporary Japan*, edited by J. E. Roberson and N. Suzuki. New York: Routledge Curzon.

Terry, Don. 1999. "Passions of Vietnam War Are Revived in Little Saigon; Shop's Ho Chi Minh Poster Sets Off Violence." *New York Times*, February 11, A–20.

Thayer, Carlyle, and Ramese Amer. 2000. *Vietnamese Foreign Policy in Transition*. New York: Palgrave Macmillan.

Thomas, Mandy. 1997. "Crossing Over: The Relationship between Overseas Vietnamese and Their Homeland." *Journal of Intercultural Studies* 18(2): 153–76.

———. 1999. *Dreams in the Shadows: Vietnamese-Australian Lives in Transition*. Sydney: Allen and Unwin.

Tolentino, Roland B. 1996. "Bodies, Letters, Catalogues: Filipinas in Transnational Space." *Social Text* 14(3): 49–76.

Tollefson, James W. 1989. *Alien Winds: The Reeducation of America's Indochinese Refugees*. New York: Praeger.

Tran, Dinh Huou. 1991. "Traditional Families in Vietnam and the Influence of Confucianism." Pp. 27–53 in *Sociological Studies on the Vietnamese Family*, edited by R. Lijestrom and T. Lai. Hanoi: Social Sciences Publishing House.

———. 1996. "Gia Dinh va Giao Duc Gia Dinh [Family and Family Customs]." Pp. 118–136 in *Nhung Nghien Cuu Xa Hoi Hoc Ve Gia Dinh Vietnam* [Sociological Research on Vietnamese Families], vol. 2, edited by T. Lai. Hanoi: Social Science Publishing House.

Tran, Xuan Nhi. 1995. "Vietnam's Families." Pp. 217–226 in *Worldwide State of the Family*, edited by A. Gafurov. Tashkent: Institute of Strategic and Interregional Studies.

Turner, Sarah, and Phuong An Nguyen. 2005. "Young Entrepreneurs, Social Capital and *Doi Moi* in Hanoi, Vietnam." *Urban Studies* 42(10): 1693–1710.

United Nations. 2000. *The World's Women, 2000: Trends and Statistics*. New York: United Nations.

———. 2006. *International Migration and Development: Report of the Secretary General*. New York: United Nations.

United States Department of Homeland Security. 2006. *Yearbook of Immigration Statistics: 2005*. Washington, D.C.: U.S. Department of Homeland Security, Office of Immigration Statistics.

United States Immigration and Naturalization Service (USINS). 1999a. *Annual Report: Legal Immigration, Fiscal Year 1997*. Statistics Branch: 1–13.

———. 1999b. *International Matchmaking Organizations: A Report to Congress by the Immigration and Naturalization Service*.

———. 2002. *Statistical Yearbook of the Immigration and Naturalization Service, 1999*. Washington, D.C.: U.S. Government Printing Office.

Wacquant, Loic. 1989. "Toward a Reflexive Sociology: A Workshop with Pierre Bourdieu" *Sociological Theory* 7(1): 26–63.

Wang, Hong-Zen, and Shu-Ming Chang. 2003. "Commodifying International Taiwanese-Vietnamese Marriages." *Taiwanese Sociology* 6 (December): 177–221.

Waters, Mary C. 1999. *Black Identities: West Indian Immigrant Dreams and American Realities.* Cambridge: Harvard University Press.

Weber, Max. 1978. *Economy and Society.* Berkeley: University of California Press.

Weiss, Robert Stuart. 1995. *Learning from Strangers: The Art and Method of Qualitative Interview Studies.* New York: Free Press.

Williams, Raymond. 1972. *Marxism and Literature.* London: Verso.

Wilson, Ara. 2004. *The Intimate Economies of Bangkok: Tomboys, Tycoons, and Avon Ladies in the Global City.* Berkeley: University of California Press.

WIN News. 1995. "Arranged Marriages the Rule in Pakistan." *WIN News* (Summer): 66.

Wisensale, Steven K. 1999. "Marriage and Family Law in a Changing Vietnam." *Journal of Family Issues* 20(5): 602–616.

Yamane, Linus. 2001. "The Labor Market Status of Foreign-Born Vietnamese Americans." Unpublished manuscript.

Yang, Mayfair Mei-hui. 1997. "Mass Media and Transnational Subjectivity in Shanghai: Notes on (Re)cosmopolitanism in a Chinese metropolis." Pp. 287–322 in *Ungrounded Empires: The Cultural Politics of Modern Chinese Transnationalism,* edited by A. Ong and D. M. Nonini. New York: Routledge.

Yang, Philip Q. 1995. *Post-1965 Immigration to the United States: Structural Determinants.* Westport, Conn.: Praeger.

Yu, Elena S. H. 1979. "Family Life and Overseas Remittances in Southeastern China." *Journal of Comparative Family Studies* 10(3): 445–454.

Yuh, Ji-Yeon. 2002. *Beyond the Shadow of Camptown: Korean Military Brides in America.* New York: New York University Press.

Zelizer, Viviana A. 2005. *The Purchase of Intimacy.* Princeton: Princeton University Press.

Zhou, Min. 1997a. "Growing up American: The Challenge Confronting Immigrant Children and Children of Immigrants." *Annual Review of Sociology* 23: 63–95.

———. 1997b. "Segmented Assimilation: Issues, Controversies, and Recent Research on the New Second Generation." *International Migration Review* 31(4): 975–1008.

Zhou, Min, and Carl L. Bankston III. 1998. *Growing up American: How Vietnamese Children Adapt to Life in the United States.* New York: Russell Sage Foundation.

Zinoman, Peter. 2001. *The Colonial Bastille: A History of Imprisonment in Vietnam, 1862–1940.* Berkeley: University of California Press.

Index

About the Author

Hung Cam Thai is an assistant professor of sociology and Asian American Studies at Pomona College in Claremont, California.